ANTONIA

FOR LOVE OF A RO

faber and faber
LONDON · BOSTON

First published in 1965
by Faber and Faber Limited
3 Queen Square London WC1N 3AU
First published in this edition 1972
Reprinted 1973, 1976, 1979, 1983, 1986 and 1989

Printed in Great Britain by
Cox & Wyman Ltd, Reading, Berkshire
All rights reserved

ISBN 0 571 10118 6

en souvenir de Francis Meilland (1912–1958)

A ta chère mémoire et ton oeuvre féconde
Ce livre est dédié. Il célèbre à la ronde
Les dons et les vertus de Ceux que tu aimais
Et l'hommage fervent qu'on te doit à jamais
Pour ces royales fleurs que pour nous tu créais
      O magicien de Roses!

Henri Fessel

CONTENTS

CHAPTER ONE

Antoine

This is not only the true story behind one of the best-loved and the most famous of all the world's roses, it is also the true story of a family; and as always happens in any real-life story, in any slice of history for that matter, it is difficult to decide just where and when and with whom one ought to begin.

However, one must make a start somewhere, and to my mind, if not to his, this family story can well begin with Papa Meilland coming into this world, protesting most lustily, or so he has been told, on a lovely June day in 1884 in the French village of Chamboeuf.

Chamboeuf is a quiet little village lost in the pleasant but not precisely breath-taking countryside some nineteen kilometres from the grimy and friendly mining town of Saint Etienne, and about fifty or so kilometres from the clean and stately city of Lyons. As far as Papa Meilland knows, nobody has ever yet been inspired to sit down and compose a few lines for any guide book, much less a poem about his village of Chamboeuf, and to be honest why on earth should they? There is nothing in the least remarkable or poetical about Chamboeuf.

Yet this is precisely why all those old songs – which one still sings in France, especially when one is feeling beautifully mellow and sentimental after an excellent meal to celebrate some red-letter occasion – every one of those old songs, from 'The Voice of the Forests' to 'The Oxen', makes Papa Meilland blow his nose to hide his emotion. One would swear the writer of every one of those songs must have been born in *his* village – a sentiment shared undoubtedly by millions of other Frenchmen born in villages all over France.

But Papa Meilland says this is not as crazy as it sounds, Chamboeuf being outstanding in one way only – it is so remarkably like a million other quiet, unremarkable villages up and down France. So every one of these rustic home-sweet-home ballads fits them all like a glove.

Moreover Chamboeuf hasn't altered much since he was a child. La Place, the heart of the village, is still there, shaded by the same friendly plane trees with the same battered benches beneath them, where one can sit and gossip when one is old; and set about La Place – the church, the café, the school, and the 'épicerie' where, in Papa Meilland's young days, one could buy all the necessities of life from sugar, salt, paraffin and slippers to an ancient panacea that positively fascinated him for it dated right back, or so one said, to the Battle of Agincourt, when it triumphantly healed all but the most mortal of wounds inflicted by the arquebuses and flying arrows of the invading English. And was still confidently believed to be the sovereign cure for all everyday wounds, not to mention coughs, colds and colic. One either swallowed a dose or rubbed it in, as commonsense or preference dictated.

But to come back to Chamboeuf. There too, still on La Place, is the Mairie, and many, many a time has Papa Meilland's patriotic young self cheered himself hoarse to behold Monsieur the Mayor of their village emerge from their Mairie on July 14th, proudly wearing his red, white and blue mayoral sash and looking and doubtless feeling ten feet taller to represent on that glorious day the majesty of the French Republic.

Other days, shrunk down to ordinary size, Monsieur their Mayor would be hard at it, working in the fields or vineyards, just like any other inhabitant of quiet Chamboeuf.

In those days, of course, Papa Meilland went by the name of Antoine, given to him in Holy Baptism with him still bawling so lustily he all but drowned the voice of Monsieur the Curé, or so his scandalised mother used to complain.

He was one of four children and his parents had a small farm, two or three cows, a couple of fields of wheat and potatoes, an orchard, a small vineyard, a large vegetable garden every inch meticulously cultivated, any number of fowls, ducks, geese and rabbits; and like everyone in those parts in those days, a fine contented pig – Seigneur Cochon, Lord Pig, to quote his father's well-worn witticism.

But don't run away with the romantic notion that life was poetically easy on that small farm. Far from it. His parents had to toil hard all the hours God gave, and even then money was eternally tight. They ate meat only on Sundays and on special occasions; coffee was even a rarer treat relished only on truly red-letter days. But don't imagine for one moment, however, that they all half-starved. Nothing of the sort. They always tucked into the heartiest, the most wholesome of meals. Papa Meilland's mother had been a cook in a grand house before she married and she knew how to work savoury miracles with the good vegetables and fruit they grew on their small farm. Indeed, no banquet yet has ever tasted half as good to Papa Meilland as the crisp golden chips his mother used to pile high on their plates flanked with a mountain of green salad; or her steaming, thick vegetable soup helped out with a thrifty salted morsel of last year's Lord Pig.

Nobody, by the way, was ever in the least sentimental about Lord Pig. Indeed, for every family in the village and for miles around it was one of the merriest days of the year when one's friends and neighbours came in to help kill the year's Lord Pig with merciful speed; and then set to work to make the delicious sausages, and the salted this and that which would last the family the whole year to come – with the utmost economy, of course. And as his father always solemnly pointed out on these busy merry days, not only did one appreciate every scrap of good Lord Pig from the tip of his tail to his fat pink cheeks, but his Lordship was always treated with every consideration. He was well fed, well housed, enjoyed the most care-free, the best of lives whilst it lasted, which was more than one could say of many a poor devil of a human being. He knew! None better. Had he not fought in the Franco-Prussian War of 1870? This bitter war may seem centuries ago to people today, but to Papa Meilland's father it seemed only yesterday; and many a winter evening did Papa Meilland sit there, his hair standing on end on his young head to hear his father tell all over again how he had been in Paris all through the terrible siege with the Prussian guns thundering away night and day, and the people of Paris falling dead of starvation and cold in the streets. And one is not fastidious when one is famished, said his father, so there was not a horse, a cat, a dog, a pigeon, a rat left in all the city; they were eaten, every one.

Maybe it was his father's memories of those cruel hungry days that made their small farm so regular a port of call for the Tuesday beggars. In those days, the local beggars, some of them talented professionals one has to admit, had a regular weekly round, calling at this or that village on set days of the week. Tuesday, it was always Chamboeuf; and never once, no matter how tight money was, never once at any time was any beggar turned away from their farm without a bowl of good hot vegetable soup and a hunk of bread spread with pork dripping. And if it was cold and night was falling, they were always sure of a warm snug place to sleep in the barn.

Then every summer, regular as clockwork, they had other and far more entertaining visitors – the Italian chair-makers. Now they were the gayest of men with swarthy faces and black dancing eyes; and such workers! They would select a cherry tree still growing in someone's orchard, chop it down, saw it up with swift beautiful precision, and in three days, just three days' time, there they would stand – one's new chairs, ready for use, and far better than any chairs one could buy at twice the price in Saint Etienne or Lyons.

These friendly Italians lived with the family they were obliging, of course. One always made room for them somewhere, and when darkness fell, but not a moment before, they would troop in to supper, washed down with a couple of bottles of wine, and then sit outside the kitchen door enjoying the cool night air. And one of them would bring out his accordion and strike up a tune and they would begin to sing, sometimes so gentle and haunting a ballad that though one could not understand a word, one's heart would melt like butter and the tears come to one's eyes. Then, the next moment, off they would go on so merry and beguiling an air that the girls would spring to their feet and soon there would be those laughing Italians teaching them to dance like so many ballerinas.

Then clear as yesterday Papa Meilland can still see his youthful self setting off for school every day in his sensible black overall, buttoned up down the back, with a belt around his waist and two handy pockets in which to stow all manner of treasures, and on his feet stout black boots with thick wooden soles, which made a first-class din as he clattered along.

Indeed, these wooden-soled boots, worn by all his pupils, may well have been the reason why poor haggard Monsieur Spécel, their village schoolmaster, only taught Physical Exercise from the waist up.

Theirs was a one-room school, you must understand, and a small one at that. And there were always thirty or so of them, all with these boots on their feet, jammed tight along the battered benches, both sexes, all ages, all sizes. And believe Papa Meilland, thirty pairs of those boots springing to attention or marking time in that one small classroom would have been enough to deafen Napoleon himself, and as heaven and history know, he positively gloried in the thunder of marching boots.

So poor Monsieur Spécel only exercised them from the waist up, and even then mostly Deep Breathing, which was understandable for it also rendered them all speechless for a while.

And why didn't Monsieur Spécel exercise his wooden-soled pupils out in the school-yard? For the simple reason there wasn't one. For recreation, he gratefully turned them all out to gallop and yell on La Place.

As for instructing them, well, the poor man did his earnest best, but everyone, everything, had to be taught in that one crowded small classroom. Moreover, harassed mothers would of hard necessity often call in and dump their two- and three-year-olds on poor Monsieur Spécel, and leave them there, kicking and yelling, whilst they hurried off to help on the land. So naturally the older pupils were always expected to lend Monsieur Spécel a hand, which they did right readily with the most ruthless severity. Indeed, Papa Meilland regrets to admit he himself has often thumped and smacked the alphabet, the numbers up to ten, the rivers of France and other useful erudition into more than one juvenile blockhead. But to be serious, when he looks back now, he marvels that, in

spite of everything, poor Monsieur Spécel managed to teach
them so much, and so well.

But far more heart-breaking than all beside for Monsieur
Spécel must have been the way that hardly one of these thirty
or so pupils was ever left at school long enough to sit for the
'Certificat d'Etudes' – 'The Certificate of Studies' – at the ad-
vanced age of twelve, and so cover him too, if successful, with
academic glory. But no, at ten, almost every one of his pupils
was already out working all day on the land, or minding the
cows, or down in the dark mines of Saint Etienne, earning
their keep, all studies forever behind them.

Now Papa Meilland's parents had never had the chance, the
luxury, of going to school, but this seemed to make his mother
all the more ambitious for her own four children. Come what
may, she was doggedly determined that all four of them should
remain at school, continue their studies until they were twelve,
and sit for that glittering 'Certificat d'Etudes'. One day, please
God, there they would be, those four certificates, framed, and
hanging on the wall side by side for all to see and admire.

Papa Meilland says he himself wasn't precisely enthusiastic
about this prolonged education of his. On the other hand,
school was no penance for him. He liked poor Monsieur
Spécel, he even liked some of his lessons, and he fully intended
to please his hard-working mother and start to slave at school
one day – later on, of course – so that he too would win his
'Certificat d'Etudes' to hang on the wall.

Meanwhile, of course, his most interesting hours were spent
outside that crowded noisy little school-room; above all the
hours, the wonderful hours he spent with Madame Mivière.

Madame Mivière, kind good Madame Mivière! Little did
she dream how she was to influence, to shape all his life.

She was the widow of a retired schoolmaster who had come
to live in quiet Chamboeuf, a homely little woman with a

pleasant word and smile for everyone. But now Papa Meilland realises that she was the most remarkable of women, years in advance of her time in her thinking, above all about children. She knew so well how to fire a child's interest and imagination, how to teach him to use the eyes the good God had given him, how to observe for himself the ever-changing wonder and beauty of the fields and forests about him.

She would let him go with her for long walks across the fields and into the forests and suddenly make him stand still and silent to watch some bird or insect; or she would point out the exquisite shape and scent of some wild flower, or the grace and colour of some spray of berries in autumn, so many familiar and lovely things he had always galloped past before, never giving them a glance, a passing thought.

She also showed him the best places to look for mushrooms, all manner of mushrooms; she taught him their names, and he still recalls with infinite delight a certain cluster of little green pine trees growing in the nearby forest, and there, at their feet, grew the daintiest, the most delicious of all little mushrooms.

But it was her garden that fascinated him most of all. He was forever hanging around her gate, whistling nonchalantly as if he just chanced to be passing by, till she would hear him and invite him to come in. She certainly had the kindest of hearts, for never once, no matter how busy she was, did she make a small boy feel a nuisance, unwanted. She always made him feel as if he was the very boy she most wished to see, for, look, here was something new and interesting just springing up, or opening into bloom in her garden.

Madame Mivière loved flowers, all kinds of flowers, but dearest of all she loved roses, the lovely, old-fashioned roses she grew in her garden. And there was no explaining it, but there was something about those roses that reached out and captivated Papa Meilland's young heart. He would stand there, looking at them, gently smelling them, lost in such wonder and delight he would have wept, but naturally he would have died of shame to betray any of this strange new emotion – apart from giving a manly sniff or two.

He can still see them, those lovely old roses in Madame Mivière's garden, her crimson 'Jean Liabaud', her golden yellow 'Duchesse de Ausstädt', her enchanting 'Rosa Noisetiana'. Ah yes, Papa Meilland still remembers the names of Madame Mivière's roses far better than the names of the poets of France which poor Monsieur Spécel tried to drive into his unpoetical young head.

And Madame Mivière, swift and delighted to sense his interest, began to talk to him of the long, long romance of the rose, telling him how, since time began, men the world over have declared their love of a rose. Study history, or travel where one may, said Madame Mivière, and time and again one comes across the most moving evidence of the way the human heart has always gone out to the rose. And he would listen to her entranced, picturing Chinese emperors long, long dead, meditating in silken state in the celestial perfume of their vast imperial rose-gardens. Or he would picture the rough seamen of old sailing the Seven Seas in their cockle-shell boats and coming home to tell how the scent of yellow roses would come drifting across the blue waters lapping the far-away island of Rhodes, making all their hearts grow soft as velvet within them.

He also loved to picture fine, swaggering Thibault, King of Navarre, galloping home from some glorious Crusade, and bringing with him cuttings of the damask roses that bloomed in the gardens of the infidel Turks to plant in his own royal Christian garden.

But best of all he loved to stand and look at Madame Mivière's 'Rosa Noisetiana', his heart going out, if you please, to the Empress Josephine, who also loved roses and who had that very rose growing in her own garden at Malmaison. And presently he would imagine he could see a great clumsy giant of a man come lumbering into Josephine's rose-garden, a man with monstrous misshapen hands, the hands of a navvy, so they said. But those hands could paint flowers, and above all roses, with such charm, such delicacy, such love, said Madame Mivière, that his paintings will always speak to the heart as well as the eye.

His name was Pierre-Joseph Redouté, and Madame Mivière, tears in her eyes, would tell how he came lumbering one day into the room where poor Josephine lay dying, two lovely flowers fresh from her beloved garden in his grotesque hands.

'Majesté,' he stammered, 'I will p . . . paint them for you.'

Madame Mivière said kind Josephine managed to smile, and she croaked:

'Then don't come too near me. You might catch my terrible throat.'

Josephine died that night of her terrible throat and the last two flowers she was ever to see were those two in Pierre-Joseph Redouté's hands. And though no history book has ever said so, something told Madame Mivière they were surely roses, maybe two delicate 'Rosa Noisetiana', just like the ones in her own little garden.

Ah yes, Papa Meilland would listen eagerly to every word Madame Mivière could tell him about Josephine and her roses, which was more than he ever bothered to do when poor Monsieur Spécel talked himself hoarse about Napoleon and his glorious battles.

But this wasn't the end of Madame Mivière's kindness to him. She would also lend him the catalogues she received every year from a professional rose-grower with gardens on the outskirts of Lyons.

Antoine

Papa Meilland can still see them, those catalogues. So dull, so bleak, so stiff they would seem to modern eyes. No glossy expensive paper, no glorious colour reproductions, indeed, no illustrations of any kind – just a list of new and old varieties of roses, with a few words of sober description, and the price of each bush or climber, all in small black print.

But to him they became the key to a whole world of enchantment. He would pore over those catalogues until he knew every rose by heart, could see in his mind every one of those trees, bushes and climbers so soberly described by that honest rose-grower.

Presently, with infinite patience, Madame Mivière began to explain to him how, down the ages, man had learned not only to propagate roses but also to 'cross' roses, marry one rose to another as it were, hoping for even lovelier children of these marriages. Her favourite 'Rose Noisetiana', for instance, was a child of a sweet-smelling American musk rose and a delicate pink Chinese rose, or so Madame Mivière had once read in a botany book. But this 'crossing' of one rose with another, said Madame Mivière, was definitely a skilled job for an expert who was prepared to take endless time and patience in his search for a new and lovelier rose.

But she herself would often experiment, striking cuttings of some favourite rose or hopefully planting the tiny seeds from the ripe rose-hips of late autumn. But far more wondrous to his young eyes she showed him the only certain and exact way to reproduce any rose – budding, she called it. She would dig up some strong young dog rose growing wild as you please in the forest, bring it home and carefully trim off all but one very short central twig, and then, using a special and very sharp knife called a 'greffoir', into this selected twig she would delicately insert and bind into place a living bud of the rose she wished to propagate. And when he saw this miracle

23

work with his own two eyes, saw beautiful roses grow and burst into bloom nourished by the roots of that obliging and hardy young dog rose, he looked down at his own two strong hands, and knew what he was going to do in life.

When he was twelve he would have to leave school and start work, of course. But not like all the other boys of Chamboeuf, not in the fields or looking after the cows, or down in the dark mines of Saint Etienne. No, no, and no.

Roses. He would work, spend all his life long among roses.

He looked at his hands again. He could never paint roses like Pierre-Joseph Redouté. Nobody could. But he, Antoine Meilland, would grow and propagate roses, beautiful charming roses, and make his living selling his rose bushes to other people. And in his spare time he too would cross one lovely rose with another and one day he would make all other professional rose-growers gasp with surprise to behold a glorious new rose created by Monsieur Antoine Meilland, Rose-grower, Chamboeuf.

Then down to earth crashed Monsieur, that future rose-grower. First, there was that fateful 'Certificat d'Etudes'. A professional rose-grower would certainly need that as well as a 'greffoir'. He would have to know how to spell, and how to describe the roses he grew for sale, and how to add up bills and write polite grammatical letters to his customers.

And there, too, was his mother. He loved her; he wanted to please her; so he simply *had* to win that 'Certificat'. And suddenly, to Monsieur Spécel's surprise, young Antoine Meilland, at the age of eleven, got down to his studies with the most gratifying ferocity, determinedly bawling away the past tenses of irregular verbs, the rivers, the ports, the heroic figures of France, past and present, and all the erudite rest a French twelve-year-old was expected to be able to rattle off as word-perfect and intelligent as some well-trained parrot if he was ever to satisfy the learned gentlemen who not only marked the papers of all the candidates for the 'Certificat' but put them through a searching oral inquisition as well.

Equally ferociously, but in silent secrecy, Papa Meilland says he began to save every sou, and there were not many of them knocking about in his young life. A rose-grower would definitely need his own 'greffoir' and a real rose-grower's 'greffoir' would cost thirty sous – all of a shilling, a fortune in those days to any child in Chamboeuf.

Nor was this all he suddenly had on his young mind. Now, too, was the time when Monsieur the Curé began to prepare the boys and girls of his age for the most solemn, the holiest day in their lives – their First Communion.

Indeed, it seemed to him that suddenly, almost overnight, he was no longer a child, and that everything which had been so momentous before, the Tuesday beggars, the Italian chairmakers, the killing and salting down of Lord Pig, everything now faded into gentle unimportance. And one memorable day he and his mother got up at crack of dawn and set off to catch the train to Saint Etienne.

Now Saint Etienne may be only nineteen kilometres from Chamboeuf, but this was his first, his very first trip in a train. Moreover, for the very first time in all his life he was to have a new suit, a completely new outfit to wear on the most solemn day of his life. Until then he had always inherited his older brother's clothes, darned and patched and cut down to his size. But now his mother had the money carefully counted out and stowed away in her worn black purse – he was positively going to blaze from head to toe, everything new, even a white handkerchief to decorate the breast pocket of that first new suit for his first Holy Communion.

Papa Meilland remembers his mother sitting by his side in the train, every bit as excited as he was, and dressed in her

decent Sunday black jacket and long skirt, a black straw hat
jammed tightly on her head, and as always, not a hair out of
place. And he remembers clutching the edge of the hard
wooden seat, watching the fields, the cows, the hedges go
rocking past at alarming speed; and how when they at last
shot into Saint Etienne his heart began to thump harder than
ever, and he felt again and again to make absolutely sure that
he hadn't lost them, that they hadn't been shaken out of his
pocket with all this speed – the thirty sous tied up tightly in
his handkerchief. He had managed it just in time, he had saved
that fortune, those thirty sous. He had even told his mother
what he wished to buy, and she had said, yes, but only after
they had decided on his new outfit of course.

They seemed to walk kilometres and kilometres up and down
the busy streets of Saint Etienne, inspecting one shop after
another. At last his mother decided to patronise the first shop
they had inspected, and then came the long careful choosing,
the minute inspection of hems and seams that would have
to be let out as he grew; and at last, at very long last, came the
splendid moment when all purchases right down to the new
white handkerchief were completed, and they made for the
Place Marengo and sat down on a bench on that pleasant busy
square to eat a picnic meal. His mother had, of course, brought
everything with her in a basket.

Any other time it would have been wonderful to sit there,
feasting on hard-boiled eggs, slices of sausage, cheese, and
hunks of good bread, looking at all those people strolling
along or hurrying home to their own mid-day meal. But now
he longed to bolt that feast; he was burning to get back to
the shops, not to the gentlemen's outfitters, heaven forbid,
but to the far more wondrous shops he had spotted here and
there that sold tools of all kinds, the splendid tools made in
Saint Etienne, the best in the world; everyone said so.

And truly those shopkeepers of Saint Etienne were the kindest, the most sympathetic of gentlemen. On that golden day they treated a lad with thirty sous to invest as if he were Monsieur the Minister of Agriculture himself about to buy up every tool in Saint Etienne. And at last, after blissfully inspecting a thousand and one 'greffoirs', he made his choice, unknotted his handkerchief, counted out the thirty sous on the counter, and carried away his 'greffoir'.

As for the journey back, he sat in the train blind as a bat to the flying landscape, intoxicated with joyous pride and satisfaction. There on his mother's lap lay the parcels, his first brand-new outfit; long trousers, waistcoat, jacket, white shirt, new shoes and socks and snow-white handkerchief. And there in his pocket, where he could feel it, was his 'greffoir'; and no other budding-knife in all this wide world has ever been so worth its weight in shining gold as that one was to future rose-grower Antoine Meilland.

Now a First Holy Communion in France is not only a most solemn occasion for a French child, it is also a great family occasion. And Papa Meilland says their relations and friends turned up, as expected, all in their best clothes, and all, as confidently expected too, bringing him a pious little present, a rosary, a prayer-book, a framed picture of Saint Antoine, and so on; and also as expected, they all admired him in his fine new suit.

They all said, too, that Monsieur the Curé preached the best sermon of his life, and just the right length, that sympathetic homely priest knowing that all the mothers of Chamboeuf and district would be piously but vainly striving to smother their anxious thoughts about the festive meal they had so carefully prepared to serve to their families and visitors once High Mass was over.

But Papa Meilland regrets to confess that he himself only heard the first sentence or so of that best sermon of Monsieur their Curé's life, the ones in which he spoke most beautifully of the good God and His peaceful heaven. However, he has the feeling that both the good God and Monsieur their Curé would have forgiven the solemn lad, sitting so still, caught up in a high celestial world of his own, busily planting, if you please, all the shining spaces of God's heaven with beautiful roses, the finest of roses, chosen regardless of cost from that rose-grower's catalogue.

Suddenly a hearty shove from the boy next to him brought him down to earth again and he too scrambled to his feet and began to sing with the others: 'Au Ciel! Au Ciel!' – 'In Heaven! In Heaven!' But as he sang he still saw them, those lovely roses he'd been planting, blooming away to the glory of God. Surely heaven could not be heaven without roses. Not without roses.

Once that pious and splendid day was over, closer and closer they seemed to loom, the ominous two days of the 'Certificat d'Etudes', the first day devoted to the written examination, the second to the even more fearsome oral interrogation. And Papa Meilland still gratefully recalls how poor Monsieur Spécel not only crammed him, educationally, to bursting point but also did his best to inspire him with confidence. But as that honest schoolmaster rightly pointed out, it might well be French Composition that would trip him up and send him, and poor Monsieur Spécel with him, headlong into ignominious failure. One always blamed the schoolmaster, mourned poor Monsieur Spécel, never the pupil – oh, never the pupil!

'And you never seem to know how to *develop* any subject, Antoine! So for heaven's sake, on this occasion take your time. Sit and THINK. Concentrate! Don't dip your pen in the ink and write your usual few sentences in your largest handwriting and imagine you will dupe the examiner into thinking that will pass for a composition. Develop the subject, Antoine, develop it! And for at least two pages.'

Poor Monsieur Spécel had put his finger right on it, of course. Papa Meilland admits that he would always sit there, chewing his pen, staring with blank dismay at orders like:

Describe a thunderstorm

or

An old proverb says: 'A good name is far better than a golden belt.' Say what you think of this statement.

There were any number of similar lofty subjects considered suitable for twelve-year-olds to develop in those days; but all he could ever manage was four or so factual sentences, and as Monsieur Spécel reproachfully said, all four in his very biggest handwriting, and then there he would sit, drained dry, not one solitary idea left in his head. Not another sentence could he ever manage to develop, no matter how he racked his brains.

All too soon, of course, the fateful day arrived and he made his second trip in a train, this time to the nearby little town of Saint Galmier. Now this pleasant little town is still well known for its excellent mineral water, but in those days there were no fewer than twenty springs there. And between them they could not only cure almost every ailment under the sun, but one could safely gulp down as much as one pleased of their sparkling water, even when one was so hot and fevered that to drink ordinary cold water would have meant sudden death – or so everyone then firmly believed.

Papa Meilland says maybe this was why it had been prudently decided that Saint Galmier was the ideal place to hold any gruelling examination; but whatever the reason, every year the two-day inquisition of the 'Certificat d'Etudes' was held in Saint Galmier for all the boys and girls from miles around. Some years, however, not one candidate from any village school would turn up. This will show you how few parents could then afford to keep their children at school to the scholarly age of twelve.

But that year there was a record number – nineteen of them – boys and girls, all agonisedly gazing down at what seemed to be acres of white paper which they had to cover with convincing proof of their prolonged studies.

Then off they went, and praised be heaven, and the diligent teaching of poor Monsieur Spécel, for the Grammar, the Dictation, the Arithmetic went off fairly smoothly.

Then it came, the perilous French Composition.

He stared and stared at it; he couldn't believe his eyes. He read it again very, very slowly to make sure he wasn't dreaming. But no, there it smiled up at him, the very subject he would have chosen himself if he had been given the chance, the one and only subject he knew he could develop, and develop, and develop:

'State which trade or profession you would like to take up, and give the reasons for your choice.'

Never before had time flown at such speed; never before had any student developed away with more ease, more eager pleasure. Not only did he list the more sober reasons for his choice of a career but he also gave the romantic ones, bringing in, if you please, those rose-loving Chinese emperors and the island of Rhodes and that fine swaggering Crusader, King Thibault; and then whisked briskly on to the Empress Josephine and the painter she befriended, Pierre-Joseph Redouté; and grandly declared that even if one could never hope to paint roses like Monsieur Redouté, how equally wonderful it would be to grow and cross roses oneself and present the world one day with a new rose as lovely as 'Rosa Noisetiana or 'Jean Liabaud' or 'Duchesse de Ausstädt'.

Ah yes, though Papa Meilland says so himself, the reasons for his choice of a trade fairly sparkled with erudite flashes, thanks to good Madame Mivière. And he was just developing the immense joy and satisfaction one feels when one has successfully 'budded' a rose when they had to hand in their papers; and he hadn't even the time to blot, much less read all he had written, or carefully correct the spelling and punctuation as poor Monsieur Spécel had implored him to do.

But maybe the examiner loved roses too; maybe he recognised a born rose-grower just because of the blots, the spelling mistakes, the eager sprawling handwriting so different from the careful writing of his Dictation; for he passed. He, Antoine Meilland, passed.

Not only that, but he had very good marks indeed. A few more and he would have come out top. As it was, a mere slip of a girl beat him to it. She was top and he was second – probably she'd had time to blot her French Composition.

Papa Meilland says poor Monsieur Spécel was radiant at *their* success; but it was the look on his mother's face he was never to forget, she positively shone with love, pride and joy. Now all four of her children had their 'Certificat d'Etudes'; hers was the only family in all Chamboeuf who had accomplished such a feat. Her dream had come true. Side by side on their living-room wall would hang those four 'Certificats' for all to see and admire.

You may find this singular, maybe hard to believe, the truth is so often perplexing, but it was only at this poignant moment that he first took a real look, his first adult look, at his hardworking mother. And he realised, with a sudden surge of love that brought a lump to his throat, all she did for them – and with one hand only.

Yes, literally, one hand. His mother only had one hand. The other had been amputated – poisoned by a vicious thorn.

But he had never before given this a thought. She always coped so magnificently, always did the work of two women with that one hand and the iron hook on what remained of her other arm. And suddenly, almost as if his careless young eyes had opened before the blaze of triumphant love and pride on her face, he realised all his mother meant to them, to every soul, every creature, on their small farm.

But did he say any of this? No, not a word, not a syllable. One doesn't wear one's heart on one's sleeve, not in Chamboeuf. Maybe it's the climate.

However, something did impel him to reveal at this moment that now he had his 'Certificat d'Etudes' he wanted to become a professional rose-grower, go and work for that rose-grower with gardens near Lyons, the one who sent the catalogues to Madame Mivière.

That did it! Just as he had always secretly feared, his father almost exploded. He thought the very idea idiotic, preposterous. And back he went, the poor man, to the famished days of the Franco-Prussian War of 1870. For God's sake, why grow roses? One couldn't *eat* roses. They were nothing but luxuries. Potatoes, wheat, cows, pigs, goats, sheep, hens, ducks, rabbits, and a hundred other living things were safer, more profitable than roses.

His mother too was more than dubious; but he dug in both his young heels, cashed in ruthlessly on his shining examination results, and in the end they agreed there would be no harm in *writing* to that rose-grower. So a packet of special notepaper and envelopes was purchased at the 'épicerie', and he sat down to compose the letter of his life, the 'open sesame' to his whole future. It had to be in his very best handwriting, of course, and as polite and grown-up in style as possible.

And not too long he decided, this rose-grower being certainly a very busy man; but, on the other hand, not too short, it would have to convince the rose-grower that this Antoine Meilland was just the lad to come and work for him. And no blots, of course, no grammar mistakes and all the full stops and commas in their appointed places.

In fact Papa Meilland says he positively sweated over that letter, and to his thrifty mother's dismay copy after copy went flying into the fire before he at last settled for:

Monsieur,

I beg you to excuse the liberty I am taking in writing this letter in the hope that you will kindly read it.

I am twelve years old and live in Chambœuf, and thus not far from Lyons.

I am happy to inform you that I have my 'Certificat d'Etudes' and that I am tall and very strong for my age.

For several years now I have decided to become a rose-grower like you yourself and I will now explain how this idea came to me.

There is a lady in our village who grows roses and she not only permits me to study them, she has also shown me how to prune, strike and 'bud' them.

This lady's name is Madame Mivière and she is one of your clients. She receives your catalogues and she kindly lends them to me. I always study them very carefully and I assure you I know the names, colours, and prices of all the roses you offer for sale.

Now I have explained all this, I must state my request. Will, you, Monsieur, kindly take me on as an apprentice? I assure you I will always endeavour to give every satisfaction, and I already have a professional budding-knife purchased in Saint Etienne.

Hoping to receive a favourable reply, I beg you to accept, Monsieur, the expression of my deepest respect.

ANTOINE MEILLAND.

It seemed three endless years, not three ordinary days, before the reply came from Lyons. And down crashed all his confident hopes, all his dreams. Oh, that rose-grower was a kindly man, he did his best to soften the blow. He explained that he himself did most of the work with only occasional help from experienced hands. But if Antoine was truly serious about wishing to become a rose-grower, he would do well to get some experience if not among roses, then among trees. And he wound up by saying that if Antoine would get in touch with him again, say in four years' time with this experience behind him, there might possibly be a vacancy . . .

Experience! But he *was* experienced. He'd said so in that letter.

And in four *years*' time! Years! Ah no, he would be all of sixteen.

He didn't weep, at least not in front of anyone. But the next day he fiercely set out to look for a job, any kind of job. Other boys of his age had already been working for two whole years and here he was with his 'Certificat d'Etudes', out of work, and with no job in sight.

And Papa Meilland says one must never laugh at the black despair of any twelve-year-old. He knows. He himself now felt the most dismal of failures in spite of his 'Certificat d'Etudes', all the more so because nobody for miles around seemed to have a job for a strong, willing boy at that moment, not even the pork-butcher of a neighbouring village, and God knows he would have hated to become a pork-butcher. But this will show you how savagely determined he was to get a job, any job, just to prove . . . But what he ached to prove he simply did not know.

Then good Madame Mivière came to the rescue. She calmly said she understood that rose-grower. His letter simply meant he hadn't the time to train an apprentice as he should be trained. As for experience, well, again one simply had to be reasonable. She herself was nothing but a self-taught, enthusiastic amateur, an untrained rose-grower if ever there was one, still making mistake upon mistake. And thank heaven, laughed Madame Mivière, that she didn't have to earn her bread by selling the rose-bushes she grew or she would be joining the Tuesday beggars.

And the more one studied that letter, the more sense and real hope one read in the rose-grower's advice. So why not do precisely what he suggested – look for a job among trees? After all, roses belonged to the great family of trees; and it was always far easier to get a job once one was *in* a job and with some experience behind one.

And look, cried kind Madame Mivière, wasn't this providential? Here in their weekly provincial newspaper was an advertisement inserted by a firm of tree-growers, arboriculturists, one called them if one wished to impress, and these arboriculturists had their plantations of trees near Saint Galmier, pleasant Saint Galmier of the twenty sparkling springs of mineral water. Madame Mivière had been there more than once, bought more than one excellent young tree from them, her lovely plum and apple trees, for instance, and all four of her peach trees. A first-class firm; she could recommend them. So why not write *them* a letter and ask if they could do with a willing hard-working apprentice with his 'Certificat d'Etudes'? They would teach him everything from A to Z about trees, and with all this excellent experience behind him any reputable rose-grower would then be overjoyed to employ him – if he had a vacancy of course.

Papa Meilland still thanks heaven he listened to good Madame Mivière, and within a month he was working among trees in pleasant Saint Galmier, all kinds of trees from homely plane trees to superb peach trees.

At first, until he was of some real help, he wasn't paid a sou, of course, but again he was fortunate. It was too far for a twelve-year-old apprentice to cycle to Saint Galmier and back to Chamboeuf every day so he lived with the family of his 'patron'. And Madame, his patron's wife, was another excellent woman who believed in serving up good square meals and sleeping in warm comfortable beds. And on Sunday, which in those days was the only day, apart from feast-days, on which one rested, he would get up at dawn and cycle home to Chamboeuf for the day. And his mother would kiss him and then anxiously look him up and down to make sure he wasn't wasting away – which he most certainly wasn't – and serve up extra-special meals and pack him off early with a neat parcel of clean shirts, socks, and underwear slung on his bicycle so as to arrive safely back in Saint Galmier before it grew dark.

And as he pedalled along the quiet country roads, he would begin to whistle and sing, thinking of the distant day when he would sit down and compose a second careful letter to that rose-grower near Lyons. And surely this time, when he was all of sixteen and with so much experience behind him, he would at last step into his dream world, the world of roses, where he would live happily ever after – just like those Chinese emperors, just like Pierre-Joseph Redouté and all those rose-loving others.

CHAPTER TWO

Francesco

Now all this while, miles away, and completely unknown to young Antoine Meilland, there was another boy who was also dreaming of spending his life growing roses, nothing but roses.

His name was Francesco Giacomo Paolino; and he declares that to understand the part his family play in this true story one first ought to know a truthful little about Calabria – 'the proud poised toe of Italy' as some poet once put it.

When confronted, however, with the 'Nouveau Petit Larousse', he somewhat reluctantly agrees that this 'Dictionnaire Encyclopédique' has made a masterly job of compressing Calabria, past and present, into precisely six truthful lines of ingenious abbreviations. He concedes that Calabria is certainly mountainous; it certainly is covered with forests; and it certainly is subject to 'tremblings of the earth', though 'tremblings' is not the pale muted word with which eloquent Calabrians with long memories would dismiss their more historic 'rockings and rollings'. Ah, no!

Then admittedly there were once bands of brigands 'infesting' the forests of Calabria but here again he would dearly have loved to see, and, better still, to hear, some of their more historic brigands if this Monsieur Larousse of French dictionary fame had dared to spit so paltry a word in their fierce faces instead of printing it in his encyclopedic dictionaries over there in safe far-away France.

But to come to the real point. This Encyclopedic Dictionary of Monsieur Larousse omits one overwhelming truth about the Calabria of his young days: one was always poor and hungry in beautiful Calabria, not every day or romantically poor, but grindingly, atrociously poor and hungry. Above all, hungry for work, just plain honest-to-God work of any kind – the Calabrians being a proud race and not given to whining and holding out an abject hand for charity. Indeed, this may be the reason why some desperate Calabrians preferred to take to brigandage.

Now Francesco's Calabrian Papa had once served seven long hard years in the Army, and as he never permitted any-one to forget this, he was affectionately, but respectfully, known as Papa the Corporal. This was just as well, for Papa the Corporal was also the head of a large family of Paolinos and he therefore had to do his military best to represent the good God in the family, this being the solemn duty of any good Calabrian Papa. But he prudently gave Mamma the charge of the family purse – Papa recognising a born financier when he saw one. Indeed, even now, after all these years, Francesco still marvels at his Mamma. God and His Holy Saints alone knew how she managed it, but not only did she contrive to feed and clothe them – after a fashion – but she patiently scraped together enough money for them all to sail, on the cheapest possible ship, of course, to that El Dorado of a little French port, Antibes.

Ah yes, after star-spangled remote New York, Antibes then glittered like a second El Dorado itself to work-hungry Calabrians. One could always find employment there; every-one said so, and regular employment too; and that meant regu-lar meals and regular cash to save, not only against some

sudden disaster from which God preserve them, but also towards that golden dream of all Calabrians: to buy some land
of one's own one day, some patch of good earth to hand down
to one's children.

Thanks then to the amazing financial genius of Mamma
Paolino, one day in early autumn – in 1892, if one must be
exact – all the Paolinos vociferously but carefully packed everything they owned in this world, and this didn't take long, and
set off to catch that cut-price ship to Antibes, Papa the Corporal, Mamma, uncles, aunts, cousins, children, all the Paolinos,
with Papa the Corporal, of course, heading the emigration,
and Mamma still clutching the family purse, now woefully
flat after counting out all those lowest possible fares on that
cheapest possible ship. But showing no sign whatever of this,
Mamma followed Papa the Corporal, head held high, proud
and stately as became a Paolino without a debt in the world
and still something left inside her purse. And keeping a
vigilant eye on all the other Paolinos carrying the parcels tied
up with string and the net bags bulging with bread, goat's
cheese, onions, sausage, figs and bottles of wine, all of which,
as Mamma sternly and repeatedly warned them, had to last
until they arrived at Antibes.

As for a roof over their heads, there were some Paolinos
by birth or marriage already over there in Antibes, but they
had not been warned of the coming invasion for the simple
reason that no Paolino had ever had the luxury of learning to
read or write. But this didn't worry them. Those other
Paolinos would at once move over and make room for them
all until they found work and a roof of their own. As Papa
the Corporal fiercely declared, once a Paolino, always a
Paolino, and let no-one ever forget that.

Papa the Corporal, as always, was right. Those other Paolinos already in Antibes shrieked with delight when they

descended upon them, and talking, laughing, weeping, and waving their arms, they slapped food and wine on the table and moved over to make room for them all. In fact, if they'd only had banners and flags they would have hung them out as well to add to the welcome.

Moreover, in less than a week every one of the family had found work. But the truth is the truth and must be told. All Calabrians were known to be desperate for work, so employers were meticulously careful not to ruin so excellent a source of cheap labour and they therefore paid Calabrians the lowest possible wages for the hardest possible jobs and the longest possible hours. But what matter? The Paolinos gratefully thanked God. They all had work, regular work.

They toiled from dawn to dusk in the market gardens growing the most beautiful vegetables – choice asparagus, the sweetest of little green peas, the whitest of cauliflowers, and tender young beans; not to mention lovely flowers such as violets, lilies, carnations and anemones, all to set on the damask-covered table of the rich English Mi-lords and Mi-ladies, who in those days came to spend the winter and spring on the Côte d'Azur in stately villas or splendid hotels with magnificent views over the blue Mediterranean.

Francesco gathered their own country was then shrouded in dank dark fog through which the poor sneezed and coughed their way, but naturally the rich and high-born, with golden sovereigns in plenty, sensibly fled to the sunny Côte d'Azur where one could pick oranges and lemons from trim green little trees, and where pink geraniums and blue pansies tumbled in riotous bloom all the warm winter through. And very glad and grateful everyone was too to welcome these generous, well-mannered Mi-lords and Mi-ladies who, it seemed, never squinted suspiciously at any bill but courteously paid up without a murmur.

Francesco

And there now, on the Côte d'Azur, out in the sun under the blue sky, helping to grow the fine vegetables, the lovely flowers for these polite and profitable visitors, were the Paolinos – all of them except one, Francesco himself, aged ten.

You may be thinking that, being only ten, he was, of course, sent off to sit peacefully on a bench in the free primary school of Antibes to learn to speak and write good French for the rest of the family. But this, if one may be permitted to be so blunt, shows how lamentably little you know of life seventy-two years ago, above all life for a Calabrian family. At ten, every Calabrian was expected, indeed, *had* to earn the food he devoured or all the others had to tighten their belts a notch tighter. However, now, to his manly fury, Mamma Paolino had taken it into her head that he was not to join all the others bending their backs in the market-gardens.

'Non! Non! Tròppo piccolo! Tròppo gracile!' declared Mamma Paolino. 'Too small! Too delicate!'

This made Francesco grind his teeth. He had to admit he was small for his age, very small, in fact, but how tall was Napoleon at ten, tell him that! Or Garibaldi?

He scowled even more savagely when Mamma Paolino declared he was going to be the golden, the privileged one of the family. He was going to have the luxury of being apprenticed to a most excellent trade, one of the most dependable of all trades. He was to become a 'calzolaio' – a cobbler. People were eternally needing to have boots and shoes mended, declared Mamma, and imagine how convenient and economical it would be to have a cobbler on hand, right there in the bosom of the family. Above all, said Mamma, it would be such a safe sheltered job in the shade.

Yes, yes, decided Mamma, it was definitely to be a sheltered cobbler's life in the cool shade for their 'piccolo, gracile' Francesco.

Francesco

Now one never argued, at least not for long, with Mamma Paolino, not with Papa the Corporal and the whole tribe of Paolinos glowering and yelling and banging on the table as if one was about to thrust an ungrateful sword in poor Mamma's heart as in the picture of Our Lady of Sorrows in their village church in beautiful Calabria.

So one summer day Francesco Paolino, aged ten, began his apprenticeship in a little shop in Antibes with a sign over the door that said:

CORDONNIER, MAITRE BOTTIER

It would, of course, be poignant now to paint a moving picture of ten-year-old Francesco languishing in a dark airless shop, but this happens to be a true story. And it seems the scowl on his young face vanished like dew before the sun when he beheld the tools, the marvellous tools of Monsieur that Cordonnier, Maître Bottier.

You must understand that a Cordonnier, Maître Bottier not only knew how to mend boots and shoes, he also knew how to make them to measure. And in less than no time Francesco was eagerly hammering and stitching away, learning like lightning, and watching, most intently watching, especially when Monsieur his Patron made a pair of boots or shoes to measure.

In all modesty one can say that the good God may have absent-mindedly made Francesco on the small side, but He had generously made up for this by giving him sharp eyes, deft hands, quick wits and the most lively of imaginations. And here now was the chance to use all four of these gifts.

This does not mean, however, that he sat there dreaming of nothing but mending and making boots and shoes. No, no. On the contrary, his head had now begun to whirl with the most beautiful and entrancing dream.

Francesco

Every morning he would get up very early so as to linger for a while in the market-place of Antibes. He would first admire the stacks of immaculate vegetables, and having saluted them as one might say, he would swiftly pass on to the scented array of flowers. Mamma mia, those flowers! But best and loveliest of all to Francesco were the roses; though this was strange, there were never many of them. The local flower-growers didn't grow many roses in those days and Francesco would wonder why not, for the very sight, the scent of roses, made his own heart brim over with love like a fountain. And he would stand there breathing 'Che bellezza! Che bellezza!' till he would hear the church clock strike. Then off to his safe sheltered job in the shade he would gallop and get down to the patching, the stitching, but all the while he would be blissfully considering his dream, his two-part dream. Yes, yes, this dream of Francesco's was neatly divided into two business-like parts.

In Part One he saw himself soon setting up in a business of his own, any old shed would do to begin with; and he would work like sixty Cordonniers, Maîtres Bottiers rolled into one, not only cobbling but also making the most beautiful boots and shoes to measure that would fit like a glove. For ladies, he decided. Yes, he'd definitely specialise in ladies' footwear. He would make the most elegant boots and shoes in glowing patent or soft kid leather with white buttonholes and beautiful pearl buttons; and he had not watched Monsieur his Patron so intently for nothing. Ah, no! He too now knew how to create the extra secret 'something' that was then captivating every fashionable lady of Antibes. As she strolled along, holding her parasol over her head to keep the sun from burning her face a vulgar brown, her long skirt had to go 'frou-frou-frou' about her neat ankles and her trim little boots or shoes had to trip along with an intriguing 'cric-crac-cric-crac'. This was absolutely the latest, straight from Paris, that built-in 'cric-crac-cric-crac'.

And this alluring feminine duet of 'frou-frou-frou-cric-crac-cric-crac' made all the gentlemen lolling on the terraces of the cafés and restaurants sit up and take notice and no mistake; not to mention the way it made other less-fashionable women turn envious heads. And Francesco knew precisely how to orchestrate that stylish 'cric-crac-cric-crac'. One had to take two pieces of leather, just so thin, steep them just so long in so much paraffin, then glue them, just so, inside the shoe or boot, overlapping them just so, and leave them to dry. And 'Ecco!' at every step one would then hear it, that delightful, that very latest 'cric-crac-cric-crac'.

Soon all Antibes would be talking of Signor Francesco Paolino's cric-crac-ing masterpieces, but once the Maestro had made a stack of money he would startle everybody, break the hearts of all his elegant clients. He would sell his prosperous business, hammers, nails, thread, beautiful leather, pearl buttons, everything – at a handsome profit of course, and say a grateful Amen to Part One of his dream.

In Part Two of his dream Signor Francesco Paolino saw himself carefully selecting and buying a few acres of land. Yes, *buying* it, like that, cash down. And there would still be the cash left over to buy *them* – the rose-bushes, the most carefully chosen of bushes. Nothing but the best would do, with beautiful shapely buds and lovely blooms and long straight stems with as few thorns as possible. And he blissfully saw himself taking infinite care of his bushes; not a weed would dare to show its ugly head in Francesco Paolino's Rose Gardens.

And every morning as the sun rose he would be out among his roses, selecting and cutting perfect buds and blooms with the dew still on them, and he would sit down on his own land, and carefully tie his roses into neat bunches, and then pack them into two large baskets and carry them down to sell in the market-place.

Soon people all along the Côte d'Azur, even the Mi-lords and Mi-ladies, would be admiring 'Paolino's Perfect Roses, guaranteed cut at dawn'.

'Set only Paolino Roses on our damask-covered tables!' they would command.

Ah yes, Part Two of Francesco's dream was roses, roses all the way. But both Part One and Part Two were a close secret between Francesco, the good God and gentle Saint Francesco d'Assisi, his patron saint. One naturally had to take Them into one's confidence.

Now this ambition to own some land of his own one day was not so grand as it may seem. The other Paolinos talked incessantly of nothing else. They, too, were highly intelligent, shrewd, and imaginative and by now they had tramped for miles after Mass of a Sunday, exploring the countryside outside the ancient walls of the little port of Antibes. And they had discovered the close-by cape jutting out into the blue Mediterranean – the Cap d'Antibes.

And 'explored, discovered' are the right words. You may find this hard to believe but in those days the Cap d'Antibes was one of the loneliest, the quietest of places. On all that lovely Cap there were only three houses, just three, lost among tangled scented forests of pines and firs that tumbled down wild and free to the sea.

And you may find this even harder to believe, but one could buy as much land as one pleased on the Cap, maybe not at 'a sou a metre' as some now so wistfully declare, but it was cheap, literally dirt-cheap. After all, as everyone said, one would need the iron courage, the bulging muscles of those brawny pioneers of old who 'opened up' the American Far West to hack down the forests, grub up a million roots, tear up the jungle of brambles and bushes, make little tracks, before one could even begin to drive a spade into that dirt-cheap land.

However, the thought of hard work never dismayed any Paolino. On the contrary, to them it was a blessing straight from heaven; but they told no one, apart from heaven, of this bold decision of theirs to own some of this land on the Cap one day. As Mamma Paolino said, let the owners catch one whisper of this, and up would soar the price of course. But steadily, week in, week out, into Mamma's purse went all their wages; but don't imagine their savings went up by leaps and bounds, not even with Mamma doing all the managing.

Mamma, you must understand, was as excellent and economical a cook as she was a financial manager, but she firmly believed in feeding a family well. So she soon mastered enough French to haggle with the best in the market-place, and it must be said, in all honesty, that once the ordinary people of Antibes got to know the newly-arrived Paolinos they all became very kind and helpful – especially to Mamma. So she always managed to secure her share of the day's 'best buys'.

Above all, Mamma dearly loved to set a great steaming dish of superb 'pasta asciutta' before her ravenous family, with Papa the Corporal presiding, of course, and declaring Mamma's 'pasta asciutta' was fit to set before Her Majesty, good Queen Victoria herself. Everyone on the Côte d'Azur spoke like this of that dignified, bereaved little monarch. They all admired and respected her, 'a true Queen', declared Papa the Corporal, in so authoritative a voice that one would imagine he regularly hobnobbed with all the Crowned Heads of Europe.

Ah yes, they always ate most regally on Mamma's 'best buys'; but even the best of bargains run away with hard-earned cash, so those savings did not go up by leaps and bounds. Far from it.

When summer came and the hot sun began to blaze down on the Côte d'Azur, the Mi-lords and Mi-ladies hurried back to enjoy the more muted sunshine of their own native land. A sun-tanned skin was not then considered a status-symbol – anything but. No lady ever yearned in those days to be brown all over like a nut. So all the hot summer long the sun-baked Côte lay quiet and still, the terraces of the cafés and restaurants deserted, the stately villas and splendid hotels empty and close-shuttered; and there was, of course, a sharp drop in the brisk profitable demand for prime vegetables and lovely flowers.

But the shrewd Paolinos had prudently prepared themselves for this slack season. This was also the time when the stately villas, the grand hotels, the cafés and restaurants carried out their yearly decorations and repairs, and any alterations and extensions. So the male Paolinos promptly became builders' labourers and plasterers – at the lowest possible wage, of course; and Mamma and the other women and girls just as promptly secured orders for repairing the straw seats of the chairs now stacked so forlornly on the deserted terraces of the cafés and restaurants – all repairs at rock-bottom prices, of course, that went without saying.

Only the 'calzolaio' of the family sat on as before in the shade working away at his safe sheltered job among boots and shoes; but dreaming, always secretly dreaming of roses.

It was just about now, too, that Mamma Paolino conceded that the Paolino women and girls could no longer go on patching the patches on their dresses. So one momentous day Mamma took time off from her chair-mending and spent an entire morning briskly bargaining for a whole roll of sensible, dark, hard-wearing material, first energetically scrubbing and rubbing it to make sure she would not be paying for a whole load of deceptive dressing, and then having, in her turn, haggled and haggled till she paid a rock-bottom price, she proudly carried off that heavy roll of material as if it was cloth of gold. Then night after night she and the other women and girls sat around the long table cutting out and tacking and stitching; and one blazing Sunday morning Mamma triumphantly led all the female Paolinos to High Mass, every one of them in identical dresses of that dark, sensible material, all cut in precisely the same way with modest high necks and long sleeves, and with none of these frills and flounces that so extravagantly eat up material.

And believe it or not, but Mamma Paolino's mass production of identical dresses for all the Paolino women and girls went on for years and years with only her new daughters-in-law presently muttering a little rebelliously. But they soon toed the family line for the simple reason that they too learned to love and respect Mamma Paolino. There was something so blazingly warm and generous about her, something so beautiful and unselfish about her boundless love for all Paolinos by birth and by marriage; and as Mamma so often declared, wait, oh wait, till they had saved enough to buy some of that land on the Cap and begun to work, not for others, but for *themselves*. Ah, then life would be different indeed.

Mamma Paolino would, however, have been flabbergasted to know that the 'calzolaio' of the family who was getting on so famously in his safe sheltered job in the shade would sit there crying Amen! Amen! in his heart to that. Life would indeed be different when he too was working for himself, first making those elegant cric-crac-ing shoes, and then, most delightful of all, working among those roses, Signor Francesco Paolino's Perfect Roses, guaranteed cut at dawn.

Francesco

And one should never say dreams seldom come true, for when he was sixteen Part One of Francesco's dream most certainly did come true. There he stood one golden morning in the doorway of a tiny shop, rented to be sure, but with *his* name painted in capitals over the door:

PAOLINO. CORDONNIER, MAITRE BOTTIER

And there, on the bench inside, lay his tools and a supply of leather; all he had to do now was wait for the clients to turn up. And as in some happy dream, the clients *did* turn up, and soon sixteen-year-old Cordonnier, Maître Bottier Paolino was hard at work mending and patching boots and shoes, and even more blissfully beginning to measure and make elegant boots and shoes that fitted like a glove and went 'cric-crac-cric-crac' most fashionably at every step.

But alas for young Cordonnier, Maître Bottier Paolino, Part One of his dream soon began to go sadly awry. His clients were not the polite and moneyed Mi-ladies who paid on the dot without a murmur. Ah no! His clients had a way of picking up a pair of boots or shoes he had just made or neatly repaired for them and slapping down another pair in sore need of repairs on the bench, and airily saying, 'Right! I'll take these now and pay for both pairs next time I come in.'

And there is something very grand and noble about giving a little bow and smiling with all one's teeth when one is only sixteen and magnificently saying, 'But of course, Madame!' or 'Certainly, Mademoiselle, at your service!' as if one has a fortune in the Bank of France.

So Cordonnier, Maître Bottier Paolino grandly gave credit to one and all, but prudently did not mention this to Mamma Paolino. Something, rightly, warned him she would have shaken him till the teeth rattled in his generous head; and then stormed off to interview, and alienate for ever, his satisfied clients.

Presently, however, the elegant boots or shoes he made to measure, on credit, no longer seemed to 'cric-crac' so musically to his worried ears. No, now they seemed to croak:

'Pas payé! Pas payé!' 'Not paid for! Not paid for!'

Later on it became a popular joke that if one's boots creaked it meant one hadn't yet paid for them, but young Cordonnier, Maître Bottier Paolino heard that ominous 'Pas payé! Pas payé!' long, long before the rest of the world.

But better gather up compassionate speed now and say that the leather merchants proved to have hearts of cold black marble. They didn't believe in boundless credit; and at the age of seventeen, Cordonnier, Maître Bottier Paolino was declared a bankrupt.

Yes, yes, a bankrupt.

Papa the Corporal, Mamma, and all the other Paolinos at first reeled and were struck stone-silent. That will tell you how the news suffocated them. Then they recovered their breath and burst into torrential speech, and there sat their bankrupt, lost in grey desolation but head held high, grimly hanging on to the knowledge that others before him had also been made bankrupt, powerful distinguished gentlemen owning banks and race-horses, men who sat up all night counting in millions. And there he sat now, in that sorrowful but illustrious company; and all through his desolate misery ran this ferocious thread of pride and consolation.

Maybe the other Paolinos caught something of this, too, for presently their angry rage fell from them, and they began to slap him on the back and tell him to cheer up and not go and slit his throat because funerals cost a packet and nobody even enjoyed them – unless, of course, the mourners were expecting to inherit a fortune. Then they had to rush back to work, and Francesco was left alone with Mamma. And he swears his good Calabrian angel promptly gave him a sharp peremptory

Francesco

nudge, for he suddenly knew that this was the moment to open his heart to Mamma; and he began to talk so eloquently, so convincingly of the glowing future there could be for someone like him growing perfect roses for sale that he positively staggered himself and his Mamma – and maybe his good guardian angel as well.

And presently his Mamma began to weep and to weaken, and even agree that he could always fly back to another safe sheltered job as a 'calzolaio' if ever he began to cough all night or show other alarming signs of galloping headlong to an early grave by working out-of-doors, exposed to all the dangers of fresh air and sunshine.

Better still, little by little, his Mamma began to understand his longing to grow roses, and his bankrupt heart lit up like a lighthouse and burned bright and warm within him. And three weeks later, at crack of dawn, ex-Cordonnier, Maître Bottier Francesco Paolino took a beautiful spade and bill-hook, second-hand, of course, but polished and sharpened till they glowed and cut like a razor, and set off for the lonely Cap d'Antibes.

But don't rush now to extravagant conclusions! Mamma Paolino still hadn't nearly enough saved up to buy any Paolino a worth-while patch of that dirt-cheap land. Heavens, no! But Francesco had rented a patch for next to nothing. He was going to pay that rent and earn his keep and gradually pay back those leather merchants by mending boots and shoes at night. But from now on, no more giving credit. Ah, no! No cash down, no boots back. Francesco was taking no risks whatever, not with Part Two of his dream.

It was a lovely morning. A warm little wind murmured and sang in the tangled wild forests of the Cap; the blue-green sea sparkled and shone. Never before had the sky seemed so blue, so cloudless, the sea so joyous, the birds so merry.

Francesco

When he came to his patch of that wild rough ground, he carefully laid down his bill-hook and spade and took a deep, deep breath of the sweet morning air. He looked about him; the whole wide world was beautiful, most beautiful and wonderful.

He knelt down and made the sign of the cross, and as he closed his eyes, for one lovely moment he beheld them, the roses, the perfect roses, that with the help of God he would grow on this land.

Then he rose to his feet, took up his sharp bill-hook, and, with his good Calabrian angel no doubt quivering anxiously over him, began to hack down his first wild tangle of bushes and briars. And heard himself singing away at the top of his voice.

And Dio mio, didn't he sound like Caruso, just like Caruso!

CHAPTER THREE

Claudia

Now at this same time, but completely unknown to anyone else so far in this story, a little girl was growing up in a quiet house on the outskirts of the clean and stately city of Lyons.

Her name was Claudia Dubreuil, but to understand *her* family, her childhood, one must first roll back the years, well over a hundred years in fact, right back to 1802, and imagine the Tête d'Or Park, on the left bank of the Rhône, and in the very heart of the city of Lyons.

The Tête d'Or Park, you must understand, was the pride and joy of the citizens of Lyons. No park up there in Paris, they contended, could hold a candle to their Tête d'Or with its wide avenues, its beautiful trees and rare bushes most artistically grouped to give the loveliest masses of colour, its immaculate beds of bright flowers, its tranquil lake and its hot-houses gay with strange tropical plants and exotic blossoms. It was a veritable oasis of peace and beauty, declared the more poetical citizens.

Now one of the humble gardeners who worked industriously from early to late in that magnificent park was a homely quiet man called Joseph Rambaux; and Joseph's special care and immense pride was that corner of the park in which the fruit trees grew, beautiful fruit trees, most lovingly cared for, a glory of blossom in spring and an almighty temptation to small boys in autumn with Mephistopheles himself beckoning behind every tree.

But dearest of all those fruit trees to quiet Joseph Rambaux were the young pear trees he himself had planted, training them to grow with branches neatly outstretched in disciplined ranks against a sunny wall so that they were most trimly ornamental, a pleasure to behold.

If you yourself love trees and are ever in Lyons, then take a walk if you can to the Tête d'Or Park, today more than ever an oasis of peace and beauty in that bustling prosperous city, and you may still see Joseph Rambaux's beautifully trained espalier pear-trees, venerable now with age, of course, but still most disciplined and lovely.

Now you would imagine that a gardener working all day in the Tête d'Or Park, and the hours were long in those days, would hurry home of an evening, thankfully pull off his boots and forget all about trees and bushes.

But not quiet Joseph Rambaux.

He would eat his evening meal with his wife and little daughter – they were both called Marie, by the way – then out he would go to work in his own garden. Many a wife would have grumbled, indeed kicked up hell, but Marie Rambaux loved her husband and she, too, loved their garden. So once she had washed the dishes, she and little Marie would go out to lend Papa a hand until it grew dark.

But there were no fruit trees or bushes growing in Joseph Rambaux's garden, not even a gooseberry bush. There were only rose-bushes, orderly rows of the gentle roses of those distant days, Provins, Bourbons, Noisettes and Tea Roses. And Joseph Rambaux loved them most dearly, every one.

Presently, however, he began to do more than grow roses for his own delight. He discovered he had the greenest of fingers and that his rose cuttings almost always 'took' and grew into excellent bushes. So he began to sell some of his spare bushes, and indeed to make a quiet little reputation for himself as a very small but first-class rose-grower from whom one could buy a bush or two with absolute confidence.

Joseph was so heartened by this modest success, and also, of course, by the modest extra cash coming in, that when a piece of land adjoining his own garden came up for sale, he sat down with Marie his wife, counted up their savings, and decided to risk buying it. After all, as Marie said, land was almost always an investment, and the city of Lyons was growing so fast that even if this new garden didn't turn out to be profitable they would always be able to sell it again, and probably for more than they gave for it.

But Joseph prudently decided to grow fruit trees on this second patch of land. As Marie said, the old proverb made sound commonsense: 'One should never put both feet into one boot.' So presently there was Joseph growing and tending fine young fruit trees on this extra land – just as he did all day long in the Tête d'Or Park of Lyons. But the difference was that now he often grew little saplings from seed on his own land and watched them grow under his expert care into sturdy young fruit trees, which he also began to sell to his trusting clients with full and friendly directions on how to care for them in the long years to come.

Even all this, however, did not cover everything Joseph had the faith, patience and courage to do in his limited free time. He was first and foremost a rose-lover, and like so many other dedicated rose-lovers before him, he too began to experiment, to cross-pollinate one rose with another, thinking as so many before him had thought, how wonderful it would be to breed a completely new rose, one that would combine, for instance, the heavenly scent of some homely cabbage of a rose with the delicate grace and exquisite colour of some scentless variety. But to breed any new rose by cross-pollination is not as simple as it may sound, and above all it most certainly is not speedy. In fact, one needs to have infinite patience.

First of all, having carefully chosen two parent-roses, one must learn to judge the right moment to begin operations. This is when one parent rose is not yet in full bloom, before its stamens are ripe, before its stigmas are open. One delicately removes all its unripe stamens, and promptly ties a little paper hat over its head to ward off the promiscuous attentions of bees and other insects with pollen from heaven only knows what unknown roses still clinging to their hairy legs. And also to ward off the wind. As every sufferer from hay-fever knows to his cost, 'the wind bloweth where it listeth', blowing with it the most undesirable pollen gathered en route.

Then one waits for the moment when the stigmas of this stamen-less rose are open and ready to be pollinated, takes off that protective paper hat, and delicately brushes on its open stigmas the pollen which one has already gathered from the ripe stamens of the other parent-rose. Then back at once must go that little hat to ward off again all bees and insects and any pollen-laden wind that may blow.

In short, one has to make quite certain that only the ripe pollen of the one carefully chosen parent-rose is permitted to fertilize the stigmas of the other.

But this is perhaps the easiest, the least exacting step in one's search for a new rose. Rose-seedlings are like the children of any one pair of human parents – they have a disconcerting and unobliging way of being all different, no two alike. More bewildering still, from one cross-pollination there can be as many as eight hundred new rose-seedlings; all offsprings of the same two parent-roses, the same pollination, and every one different from the rest.

So one has to select, as best one may, a batch of the most promising. But even these are always delicate and capricious, demanding constant observation and attention if they are to survive. Then, in the end, when they at last come into bloom, these new roses may only prove promising, just promising, nothing more.

So again one has to select the best, the most promising of them all, and cross-pollinate it with yet another carefully chosen parent-rose, praying that this will work the miracle, produce the lovely new rose with that unique 'something' about it, the new rose one already sees so vividly – but in one's mind alone.

But again, not one in the next vast family of new rose-seedlings may come up to one's dreams; and the whole patient slow process may have to be repeated again and again, often for years, before a truly worth-while new rose at last blossoms before one's eyes.

Yet imagine it. There was Joseph Rambaux working hard all day as a gardener in the Tête d'Or Park of Lyons, coming home to work among his own fruit-trees and beloved rose-bushes, and still finding the time, and the infinite patience, to breed one new rose after another – ten in all. But nobody outside their family and friends knew about Joseph's ten new roses. Budding was known then, but it still had to be proved to be the best, indeed the only dependable way of propagating a new rose. But even patient Joseph Rambaux could not find the time for this. So those ten new roses bloomed only in his own small garden.

The busy days, the years sped by, and all the while Joseph's little daughter, Marie, was fast growing up, of course. But before that happy gardener had time to observe this, his wife was plaintively demanding to know if he had eyes in his head for anything but his roses and fruit-trees; and hadn't he noticed it even now? What? For heaven's sake, the way young Francis Dubreuil, the tailor, was forever making all manner of excuses to call in and admire their roses when it was clear as the nose on one's face that what he really admired so much was their Marie, yes, their daughter, Marie.

It was true. In next to no time young Francis Dubreuil was asking to marry their pretty little Marie, telling Joseph honestly and precisely just how much he made as a tailor, proving conclusively he could now afford to marry, and, most important of all, assuring Joseph he would make the most loving and faithful of husbands.

And there was their quiet little Marie determined not to wait but to marry Francis Dubreuil without delay or immediately die young of a broken heart. And Marie was not only an only child, she was also delicate, always a little ailing with this or that. So, bewildered and alarmed, Joseph had to adjust himself to being old enough to have a married daughter, and to becoming papa-in-law to young Francis Dubreuil, the tailor.

And if this wasn't enough, just one short year later, didn't the pair of them present Joseph with a grandchild, a beautiful little girl whom they christened Claudia.

Now don't imagine for one moment that kindly Joseph Rambaux didn't take to Francis Dubreuil as a son-in-law. No, indeed. It was simply the way time had whisked along and he all unawares of its flight, till there he was a grandpapa. Say what one likes, that does sober a man, make him realise just how elderly he is.

Joseph, in fact, truly liked Francis Dubreuil. He was a quick-witted, clever young man; and this, of course, went to Joseph's heart, his son-in-law soon proved that he really did love roses. Every day when he had done with the cutting, the tacking, the fitting of his gentlemen clients, he would spend happy hours with Joseph in the rose-garden, helping to 'lift' the bushes to sell to the customers, learning to prune and to 'strike' them as efficiently and lovingly as Joseph himself. He even mastered the technique of 'budding' with startling success. So all in all Joseph could not have wished for a more congenial, a more helpful son-in-law, or a better husband for Marie, a more devoted papa for little Claudia.

And he was forever admiring Joseph's ten new roses, saying again and again, 'But I assure you, you simply ought to propagate them, put them on the market. People would love them.'

However, there never seemed to be the time to propagate and market these ten new roses, not with Joseph's regular job in the Tête d'Or Park, and the steady sale of old tried favourites to his faithful customers. However, one day Joseph promised himself he *would* find the time. With the help of Francis he would 'bud' his ten new roses and put them on the market; maybe even bring them to the attention of famous professional rose-growers. Yes, one of these days, that was what they would do.

That day never came. Joseph Rambaux was taken ill and died as quietly and courageously as he had lived. And all their safe, tranquil little world seemed to crumple about his grief-stricken family.

Once they had recovered a little from the shock, but not their sorrow, they had to sit down to consider the future. What now was to become of Joseph's rose-gardens, his orchard of fine young fruit trees, the modest but steady little business he had worked so hard to build up in his free time? And un-doubtedly led and fired by Francis, they decided to take their courage in both hands and do what Joseph himself would have been most moved to see them do.

It was decided that Francis was to give up his good safe job as a tailor. He was to take over and do his utmost to extend Joseph's modest rose and fruit-tree business with his widowed mother-in-law and his wife, Marie, to help and encourage him. How could they see the dedicated work of Joseph's whole life-time be taken over by strangers? No, it was unthinkable. So they took the plunge.

And this was how Francis Dubreuil, the tailor, became a professional rose-grower, though he, too, just as Joseph had done, prudently went on growing and selling fine young fruit trees as well as roses. But again, like Joseph, his real love was all for roses, and when the little business began to grow and prosper, he promptly bought more land, and on this he grew still more roses. Moreover, even with all this extra hard work and responsibility on his shoulders, he found the time to do what Joseph had never managed to bring about: he success-fully budded and propagated a collection of eight of Joseph's new roses. But before he had time to bud the last two, a second black grief rocked their lives. Marie, Joseph's widow, was also taken ill, and quietly died.

And maybe this was Francis Dubreuil's way of showing his love and respect for his kind and homely parents-in-law, but he worked harder than ever, did not rest until he had budded and propagated the last two of Joseph's ten new roses.

One was his mother-in-law's favourite, a sweetly scented yellow rose with a soft orange-gold heart and lovely foliage. She herself had named it, 'Perle d'Or', 'Golden Pearl'.

The last of Joseph's ten new roses was also yellow, but a yellow that subtly shaded to a warm delicate pink, and it too was most sweetly scented. And Francis Dubreuil called this enchanting rose:

'Souvenir du Rosiériste Rambaux'.

'Souvenir of the Rose-grower Rambaux'.

Soon bushes of one or the other of Joseph's ten new roses were blooming in many a French garden. But this was all of eighty years ago and to-day one rarely sees any of Joseph's roses listed in any rose-grower's catalogue. Over the years, like so many other lovely things, they faded out of fashion. But surely some must still bloom, names all forgotten, in some quiet undisturbed corners of old gardens, still climb scenting the summer air over some cottage wall. And one feels that homely Joseph Rambaux would have wished for nothing better; asked for no lovelier memorial.

Clever, hard-working Francis Dubreuil soon began to make a name for himself as a first-class professional rose-grower. He also began to find the time to attend professional meetings and conferences for he dearly loved to meet other rose-growers, talk to them by the hour, exchanging ideas and views; and, of course, this being France, they would all enjoy a festive meal to wind up these professional occasions.

But try as he might to persuade her, his wife, Marie, would never go with him to any function whatever. She had always been delicate, shy with strangers, and now both her parents were dead, she gradually became one of those gentle but obstinate semi-invalids, never really well, never really ill, always sending for pamphlets and trying out samples of well-advertised patent medicines; and above all never feeling able to entertain visitors or to go out to visit anyone, not even the friendliest, the most considerate of neighbours.

Year by year she grew quieter and quieter, content to potter around doing the cooking, the housework, but nothing else, nothing at all. And the only way not to distress her, to fluster her, bring on one of her 'migraines', was to humour her, seal off their home as it were in tranquil isolation and solitude.

You would imagine then that their daughter, Claudia, their only child, growing up in such an atmosphere, would rapidly have become restless, even resentful, especially as she herself was so very like her father. She, too, was full of energy, warmly imaginative, loving to meet people, to learn something of the busy world outside their own quiet home, rose-gardens and orchard.

But Claudia had the kindest of hearts and she truly loved and pitied her delicate quiet Maman. So as soon as she was old enough, she began to take on more and more of the cooking, more and more of the housework. And her Maman thought this only right and proper, and silently sat back, and, of course, became more and more delicate, more and more engrossed in her own health.

Fortunately, Claudia was never at a loss for something to do once the cooking and housework were done. She soon began to make all her own clothes, to embroider most beautifully the voluminous nightgowns, chemises, drawers and petticoats worn by all women and girls in those days. Then she also loved to help her Papa in the rose-gardens, and presently he began to trust her to prune, and even to bud their roses.

But best of all, Claudia loved to make bunches of the roses they grew, delighting in choosing colours that between them made a lovely enchanting harmony. Perhaps, dearest of all, she loved the yellow roses, the primrose-yellow and golden ones, and the ones that shaded into a delicate apricot. She would stand and look at these, lost in delight, and then expertly cut and most beautifully arrange them in some vase or bowl. But no matter what colour roses she chose, never once was there any harsh discordant note, anything banal about Claudia's arrangements. They were always delightfully original, with a scented charm all their own.

Her Papa, of course, was naturally proud to see the roses he grew so beautifully displayed and he began to bring in this and that client to admire Claudia's bouquets. And soon these admiring clients began to ask if Claudia would make special bouquets to set on the table for weddings, First Holy Communions, and other red-letter family occasions. And they were always ready to pay generously for these; and this extra money came in very useful, for no rose-grower, no matter how hard-working and enterprising, could ever hope to make a fortune – not in those days.

Then Claudia loved school, but with her Maman so delicate everyone thought it only proper that she left school when she was twelve – with her 'Certificat d'Etudes' of course. And by the time she was fourteen she was proving so reliable, so sensible, coping so well with the cooking, the housework, the work in the rose-gardens, that she was permitted to do something she had always longed to do.

All through the rose-blooming season, she would wake up just before dawn, dress herself and creep noiselessly down the stairs – so as not to awaken her poor Maman, of course. Then she would tiptoe around the living-room, setting the breakfast things on the table, and at last steal out into the cool, the wonderful dawn. Up and down the rows of rose-bushes she would go, swiftly selecting and cutting roses and buds just the right length so as not to mutilate and weaken the bushes; and then sit down on a wooden stool before a scented dewy mountain of roses, and begin to bunch them, twelve roses to each bunch; and these she would most lovingly stack into three large wicker baskets.

Then she would go to the stable where they kept their mule, Bichette, and coax her out to be harnessed to a little cart, lift up her baskets of roses, arranging them so the blooms would not be bruised by the jolting of the little cart. And up she would jump, and with a 'Oops! Oops! En route, ma Bichette!' off they would trot to the nearest local market, an open-air one on the Quai Saint Antoine, where the housewives of Lyons could always buy the freshest of country vegetables, and butter and eggs, and farmhouse cheese and freshly-picked herbs, not to mention plump chickens and fat, tender rabbits.

Now the Quai Saint Antoine was three good kilometres away and to Claudia there was something most exhilarating, most lovely, to go trotting along the quiet country roads in the fresh sweet morning air with the birds chirruping and singing as if calling 'Bonjour, Claudia! Bonjour, Bichette!' And with no-one to hear her and think her crazy, Claudia would begin to sing, too, or she would talk away to good little Bichette and tell her stories.

'Ah, Bichette, you'd never believe a story I read the other day, a true story but exactly like a fairy-tale, about a girl just my age who lived in a city in a land far-away to the north called Sweden. And listen, Bichette, this girl was so poor, so terribly poor, she had to sing in the streets in all the wind and rain, praying in her heart for some kind passer-by to throw her a copper to buy a crust of bread. And she had the most beautiful voice, Bichette, sweet as a nightingale, but people would hurry past, head in the air, saying it oughtn't to be allowed, sending children out in rags to sing in the street. All the same, some of the kinder ones would toss her a copper.

'Then, imagine it, Bichette! One day, along came a great musician and stood there spell-bound, amazed, to hear that ragged girl singing so sweetly. And straightaway he took charge of her and taught her to sing so beautifully that she became a famous prima-donna, enchanting theatres packed with people all over the world. And they called her the "Swedish Nightingale", but her real name was Jenny, Jenny Lind.'

And Claudia would lift up her own young voice and pretend to be Jenny Lind singing away in the wind-swept streets of far-away Stockholm.

Presently she would drop pretending to be Jenny Lind or some other fascinating personage in a story she'd read, for they would now be arriving on the Quai Saint Antoine already bustling with movement and noise, and with everyone recognising Claudia and her little cart filled with baskets of roses, and merrily calling out 'Ah, bonjour la petite!' as they trotted past.

Then Claudia would tether Bichette to a handy tree, her deserving head well down in her nose-bag munching her breakfast, and she would lift down the baskets of roses, arrange them on the edge of the pavement, and wait for the customers.

She must have made a picture, standing there with her baskets of roses, that eager friendly fourteen-year-old girl with her lovely dark eyes and hair and a warm smile that lit up all her sensitive clever face. And nothing was too much trouble for her. She would most willingly turn over her bunches of roses, hold out one after the other for inspection, finding just the colour a customer liked best, for nothing pleased her more than to see them walk away, smelling their roses, obviously delighted with them.

Once the roses were all sold, Claudia wasted no time but immediately set her empty baskets back on the little cart, untethered Bichette and with another 'Oops! Oops! En route, ma Bichette!' up she would jump and away they would go with many a stallholder calling a friendly 'Au revoir, ma petite!' as they trotted past. Claudia would dearly have loved to linger on the busy Quai Saint Antoine but she couldn't keep her Maman waiting too long for her breakfast. And all that day long, if Maman's head wasn't making her suffer too badly, Claudia would talk away about all she had seen and heard that morning, for nothing escaped her, she was so interested, so observant, so warmly delighted with the talk, the smells, the arguments, the laughter that always make a French street market so entrancing a place. And her Papa would laugh and cry, 'Heavens above! One would imagine the girl had been spending the day up there in Les Halles, the great markets of Paris!'

On the very rare occasions her Maman could be coaxed to spend a Sunday afternoon out in the fresh air in the stately Tête d'Or Park, in Lyons, Claudia would stand lost in pride before her Grandpapa Rambaux's famous espalier pear-trees. But this was nothing compared to her pride when her own Papa, Francis Dubreuil, after long years of patient cross-pollinating one rose with another, began to bring out his own new roses, though to tell the truth Claudia secretly did not care for the grandiloquent names he chose for them, dedicating them to the great personalities of those days: Marquise de Vivenne, Duchesse de Bragance, Princesse de Sagan, Baronne Piston de Saint Cyr and other high-born people, all of whom Claudia couldn't even imagine, they lived in so glittering another world.

All except one – Sarah Bernhardt. Claudia, who had never been farther than Lyons, never been to any theatre whatever, could easily imagine the 'divine Sarah', so tall, so very thin, and with so golden a voice that she could move theatres packed with Parisians to tears, and as everyone said, Parisians are not given to weeping easily. Claudia always devoured every word the newspapers printed about Sarah, how she loved all animals, how she had once spent one thousand francs on bread to feed the hungry sparrows of Paris, how, in fact, she always spent all her money like water just as she gave all of herself to everything she did, saying, 'It is in spending oneself that one becomes rich.'

Ah yes, Claudia adored the 'divine Sarah' – on whom, of course, she had never set eyes. And when her Papa brought out another lovely new rose, a splendid and regal purple-scarlet with the most fragrant but elusive of scents, one would almost say of Parma violets, something made Claudia exclaim: 'Sarah Bernhardt! Papa, call this one Sarah Bernhardt!'

Claudia

Now, a rose-grower never calls a new rose by someone's name – at least not someone still living – without first courteously asking permission. So off to Paris went a polite letter from Rose-grower Francis Dubreuil to great Sarah Bernhardt in Paris, describing his new rose as best he could, and begging to have the honour of naming his vivid and glowing new rose after so vivid and glorious an artiste.

And the 'divine Sarah' was precisely, but precisely, as Claudia had always imagined her. She was so generous, so warm-hearted, she didn't even wait to sit down and scribble a note. She at once sent back a telegram:

I most warmly thank you, Sir, for this delightful and moving compliment. I shall indeed be honoured to become godmother to your lovely new rose. A thousand friendly compliments.

SARAH BERNHARDT

A very great treasure, that telegram! And Claudia, who loved to keep all the family papers in neat order, laid it flat and smooth between two layers of tissue-paper, the most important paper of them all in her young eyes. And there it still is, that very telegram, yellow now, of course, with age, but still a family treasure.

Once again, however, one never seems to be able to find a mention of that purple-scarlet rose with its subtle scent of violets in any modern catalogue, but surely somewhere in some old gardens a 'Sarah Bernhardt' still blooms, forgotten by name perhaps, but still as enchanting and vivid as the memory of the golden-voiced 'Divine Sarah' herself.

When she was about fifteen, Claudia persuaded her Papa that it would be a real way to save time, and it would also look so much more professional, if she could begin to type all his business letters. So why not invest in a typewriter? She could soon teach herself to type, and the typewriter could stand on a table in the small room her Papa already used as an office; and with the door closed, the tap-tap-tap would not get on Maman's nerves.

So Rose-grower Francis Dubreuil bought his enterprising daughter a typewriter, and a cumbersome massive affair it would look now to modern eyes, but Claudia thought it absolutely marvellous; and with the help of a 'Teach Yourself' booklet she was soon able to type swiftly and accurately.

Then she set to work to teach herself shorthand – 'La Méthode Prevost-Delaunay', also from a 'Teach Yourself' book. And presently her Papa could dictate letters to send to his clients and Claudia would take down every word in Prevost-Delaunay Shorthand, and then type it all as speedily, or so her admiring Papa would declare, as any secretary to a lawyer up there in Paris.

The typewriter soon came in even more useful. For some years now her Papa had been sending out modest printed catalogues in which he listed not only the old well-tried favourites but also the new roses he and his father-in-law, Joseph Rambaux, had originated; and now Claudia began to type the addresses of their clients on the wrappers of these catalogues when they arrived from the printer. And as she typed she would imagine the people receiving the Dubreuil catalogues. For instance, there was one regular client Claudia often wished she could meet, she liked the peaceful sound of her name as well as that of her village. It was:

> Madame Mivière,
> Chamboeuf,
> Loire.

Yes, it was good Madame Mivière who had been so kind to young Antoine Meilland, who had taught him to use the eyes the good God had given him, and to love roses as dearly as she herself did. And Claudia's father, Francis Dubreuil, once a tailor for gentlemen, was the professional rose-grower near Lyons to whom twelve-year-old Antoine had so optimistically written asking to be taken on forthwith as an apprentice. It was the Dubreuil Catalogue, lent to him by good Madame Mivière, over which Antoine had pored till he knew every name, every colour, every price of the roses Claudia's father grew in his rose-gardens.

Now call it the Hand of God or Fate or what you will, but when Claudia was sixteen her Papa began to say he could do with more regular help in the rose-gardens and their orchard of fruit-trees. But they couldn't possibly afford a decent living wage for a man with a wife and children to support, so it would have to be someone young and single but strong and willing, of course, and most important of all, someone with some real experience so he could be left to get on with a job without time-wasting constant supervision.

At that very moment, out of the blue came a polite letter from the ideal young man. He wrote that he had applied to Monsieur Dubreuil, asking to be taken on as an apprentice when he left school, with his 'Certificat d'Etudes' four years ago. Monsieur Dubreuil might possibly remember that he had replied, kindly advising him to gain some experience first among trees.

He had taken that good advice, and had just finished serving his four years' apprenticeship with an eminent arboriculturist of Saint Galmier. The young man could supply an excellent testimonial from this arboriculturist and he could assure Monsieur Dubreuil that he was, indeed, experienced now in everything to do with tree-growing.

Would there be a vacancy for him in the near future in Monsieur Dubreuil's Rose-gardens? He enclosed a stamped addressed envelope and earnestly hoped to receive a favourable reply to this second application. Meanwhile, he begged Monsieur Dubreuil to accept the expression of his deep respect, and signed himself: Antoine Meilland.

And that, says Papa Meilland, is how he at last walked into those rose-gardens near Lyons – and also straight into the life of Claudia Dubreuil. But all he recalls about that memorable day is standing there, triumphantly thinking that here he was, all of sixteen to be sure, but here he was, at long, long last, working among roses, hundreds, thousands of roses. But not being one of these golden-throated Italians he had to make do with whistling joyous as a lark as he gently and expertly 'budded' the first rose-bush of his professional life.

And all Claudia was to recall about that red-letter day was how she stood at an open bedroom window, shaking out a duster, and wondered who it was whistling down there in the rose-gardens. It must be the new hand, of course. And suddenly she felt glad to hear that merry young whistling. Indeed, it was so infectiously happy and gay that she, too, began to whistle, but very softly under her breath, of course, so as not to outrage and shatter the nerves of her delicate little Maman.

CHAPTER FOUR

Marie-Elisabeth

At the very time those two young rose-growers, one whistling joyous as a lark up there near Lyons, the other singing away like Caruso down there on the Cap d'Antibes, were taking up their first professional spades, a dainty little girl of twelve was setting out to apply for *her* first professional job in the scented little town of Grasse, hidden away in the foot-hills of the Alpes Maritimes that shelter the sunny Côte d'Azur.

At least Grasse was hidden away in those days, and it was truly scented for the hills for miles around were neatly terraced so that the jasmine growing on every one of them might enjoy all the sunshine possible. Jasmine, you must understand, is the foundation of even the best, the most costly of perfumes, and Grasse was, and still is: 'The Enchanting Capital of Bewitching French Perfumes' – to quote a lyrical old guidebook.

But it wasn't only the jasmine growing on those terraced hills, the air of Grasse was also sweet with the scent of lemon and orange trees, carnations, violets, freesias, and best of all to that little girl, the most scented of roses from which is made that most romantic of all perfumes – Attar of Roses, worth a fortune a drop and so only sprinkled, or so she imagined, on the lace-edged handkerchiefs of Kings, Queens, Emperors, and American millionaires.

Marie-Elisabeth

The name of this imaginative little girl was Marie-Elisabeth Greco and both her parents worked full-time in one of the most famous perfumeries of Grasse. But even with both of them working long hours six days of the week, 'one was not rich' as her Maman so often protested, especially when the question of Marie-Elisabeth's one sou a day cropped up.

Now Marie-Elisabeth was an only child, so her Maman naturally spoiled her a little, and every day she was given this sou to buy either two slices of sausage or a bar of chocolate to eat with a hunk of bread for her 'goûter' – the traditional snack of all French school-children which staves off their youthful hunger between their mid-day meal and their supper.

The trouble was that when she came home every evening from the Perfumery, Marie-Elisabeth's Maman was always so curious to know just which one of the two Marie-Elisabeth had bought that day with her sou – the sausage or the chocolate. And Marie-Elisabeth wasn't a good liar and she was never able to evade this maternal grilling. And there was a certain beggar who was always sitting on the pavement, hand piteously outstretched, as Marie-Elisabeth skipped along to school of an afternoon so full of her Maman's good 'ravioli' or 'pissaladiera' that she felt she simply couldn't be hungry again for hours and hours. And there would sit that beggar, looking most artistically famished, grimy hand piteously outstretched.

So when her Maman would impatiently repeat, 'Well? Come on! Which was it? Sausage or chocolate?' Marie-Elisabeth would stammer: 'Maman, just imagine, there was a poor hungry beggar . . .' And at once her Maman would throw up both arms and scream that poor beggar probably had a row of houses, or as good as, tucked away in some bank. And once again she would cry, 'And one is not rich, I tell you! One would imagine you were some little Rothschild.'

Marie-Elisabeth

Then Marie-Elisabeth had another problem on her mind besides that persistent beggar. She would never admit it, but she was very short-sighted and she loathed the idea of wearing spectacles on her nose, or sitting in the very front row of her class where Mademoiselle her Schoolmistress would at once spot every diverting little distraction as it were. So she always had a convenient headache or a vague pain in her stomach the afternoons one studied geography, for instance, just in case she was ordered out of her safe back row and commanded to wield a long white stick and point out this or that city or river or mountain range on the map of France slung over the blackboard. Marie-Elisabeth couldn't even spot PARIS all in capitals on the wretched, crowded map, much less the one capital letter that would give a girl the clue to the names of lesser towns such as Nancy or Rouen. And she wasn't going to be laughed at by all those other sharp-eyed girls, so she would stay home on geography afternoons with her obliging headache or vague pain in her stomach.

She felt safer, of course, but never precisely enthusiastic about most other lessons when she could stick her head deep in a book deaf as a post to Mademoiselle her Schoolmistress crossly crying, 'Marie-Elisabeth Greco, how many times have I to tell you to sit up straight!'

No, one cannot say Marie-Elisabeth was one of these eager scholars. She didn't even want to be, not at the price of wearing spectacles on her nose.

All too soon, to Marie-Elisabeth's mind, the question began to crop up more and more frequently of what kind of job she ought to take up when she left school. Even an only child had to start working seriously and steadily then.

At first they thought of dressmaking – a good well-trained dressmaker could always make a living, and Marie-Elisabeth adored lovely clothes. She herself was extremely pretty, very dainty and small for her age, and her Maman always managed to dress her in the most attractive of little dresses and frilly pinafores. But pretty dainty Marie-Elisabeth was not feather-brained. She certainly would have loved to learn to make the beautiful trailing tea-gowns, the charming chiffon and lace blouses worn by the rich Mi-ladies who came to spend the winter and spring in sunny Grasse. But all these enchanting clothes were always sewn by hand, every tiny tuck, every fragile flounce, all exquisitely hand-sewn. And this would most definitely mean wearing those detestable spectacles on her nose.

Ordinary plain dressmaking, of course, would have put no undue strain on Marie-Elisabeth's eyesight, but she could not endure the thought of sitting before some ugly sewing-machine, endlessly treadling away, stitching the seams of sober sensible dresses in stout dark useful materials that said nothing at all to her, nothing whatever.

No, no, for twelve-year-old Marie-Elisabeth the future simply had to be among lovely things, beautiful colours, soft delicate materials. Very well then, if she couldn't sew them without wearing those frightful spectacles, she would iron them. Yes, *iron* them.

There was, you must understand, a certain most exclusive Ironing Establishment in Grasse and Marie-Elisabeth had always admired the superior young ladies of this Establishment who went tripping haughtily along the more fashionable streets of Grasse on their way to some distinguished client's stately villa or magnificent hotel, reverently carrying at arm's length, so as not to crease it, a most exquisite blouse or a lovely gown, perfectly laundered, and most beautifully ironed, not a wrinkle, not a pucker anywhere. And she had watched these superior young ladies, confident as you please, walk straight through the splendid gates and into these luxurious abodes – 'Servants and Tradesmen's Entrance', of course, but in they went and up to the splendid bedrooms, soft carpets all the way so one said, to deliver personally these beautiful creations.

Ah yes, that exclusive Ironing Establishment was wreathed in glamour to twelve-year-old Marie-Elisabeth. So there she sat on that long-ago day on the very edge of a chair, nervously waiting to be interviewed by the proprietor, Madame Rondel.

Ah, stately regal Madame Rondel! One could write a whole book about her alone. Only to gaze on her, and one instinctively knew that her Ironing Establishment must be the most exclusive in all Grasse, that Madame Rondel only had the most distinguished clients on her books. Above all, Madame Rondel had once had the privilege, the honour and glory of washing and ironing for Her Majesty, Queen Victoria, and all her entourage, when that sad, dignified little Monarch had snatched a respite in sunny Grasse from the driving sleet and fogs which swirled, or so one devoutly believed, above all Her Majesty's draughty palaces the whole British winter long.

To have had her Impeccable Majesty, Queen Victoria, as a client had naturally shed its regal lustre on Madame Rondel. Everything in her Establishment had to continue to be absolutely impeccable, and that included all her young ladies, their characters as well as their skill, industry and devotion to duty.

Marie-Elisabeth walked home that day head held high, very stately and dignified, as if something of Madame Rondel had rubbed off on her too, as it most certainly did on all her other young ladies. Madame Rondel had graciously accepted her; she was to begin work on Monday, but not on those heavenly blouses and gowns. She was to work her industrious way up to them via the dusters, the tea towels, and then if absolutely satisfactory, she might be promoted to the handkerchiefs, the linen towels and the table-napkins. Then, if she continued to give every satisfaction she might be trusted, perhaps, with the simpler embroidered chemises and drawers and petticoats.

Marie-Elisabeth

Ah yes, the path to the delightful gowns and négligés was jealously graduated in Madame Rondel's Establishment. Promotion was slow, and on merit and industry alone.

So on the following Monday, Marie-Elisabeth, aged twelve, began her professional ironing career, attired in a spotless white overall like all the other young ladies, busily ironing away from eight in the morning until ten at night. Yes, yes, ten at night; with two generous hours off to go home and linger over their mid-day meal; and all day Sunday free as air for their devotions and relaxation.

A seventy-two hour week for a child of twelve. But nobody turned a hair. Everyone, children as well, worked long hours in those days.

As they ironed away, a most decorous silence reigned in the Ironing Establishment save for the clatter of the irons, the hissing of steam, and the majestic voice of Madame Rondel. Not a word, not a whisper, was permitted from any young lady except of course an occasional polite 'Oui, Madame. Non, Madame,' to some query from Madame Rondel herself. Her Establishment was not one of those vulgar laundries eternally echoing with shrill voices and coarse careless laughter. No, indeed! One ironed in religious silence until the church clock boomed eight of an evening. At the eighth and last boom, but never a second before, the young ladies were graciously permitted – not to chatter, heavens no! – but to sing.

At eight o'clock no distinguished client was likely to be riding past, they would all be sitting down to their seven-course dinners. And singing in chorus kept the young ladies alert and awake. This was highly important; a sleepy young lady might possibly scorch something and that would be unthinkable in Madame Rondel's Establishment. But singing made no demands whatever on one's powers of concentration or one's intelligence unless one was an operatic artiste, of course.

Marie-Elisabeth

So at the last boom of the church clock striking eight, up and away soared the voices of Madame Rondel's young ladies like so many song birds that had been caged all day. 'O sole mio!' they carolled, and 'Mimi Pinson' and Marie-Elisabeth's two favourites, both of them most touchingly sentimental. One went, 'No, one could not say she was lovely, but oh, in her eyes was a glimpse of the skies' and the other was even more poetic, all about a girl who was 'born one beauteous May morn' and everyone who beheld her cried she was sweet, lovely and pure as white lilac. So naturally the refrain ran:

> *Lilas blanc,*
> *Joli bouquet de lilas blanc.*

Moreover, every verse of this song took one a stage further in the sweet, pure life of that lilac-like girl, right up to her early and fragrant death, so that the last pious refrain brought a lump to one's throat:

> *Lilas blanc,*
> *Divin bouquet de lilas blanc.*

Marie-Elisabeth, singing away with the other young ladies, naturally longed to have a romantic young lover one day who would write a song like that about her; but on second thoughts she would decide to skip the early fragrant death, and live to a lively old age.

Then life certainly had its exciting and most unusual moments in Madame Rondel's Establishment. For instance, one of Madame's regular and most valued clients was Madame la Baronne Alice de Rothschild who had the most sumptuous villa in Grasse with acres of gardens and a whole army of gardeners. And Marie-Elisabeth can still see the beautiful but simple silk blouses worn by Madame la Baronne. They were all, simply all, of precisely the same colour – a lovely muted shade of golden yellow with stiffly starched collars and cuffs of spotless, gleaming white linen. They required the most expert ironing, those blouses, you can take Marie-Elisabeth's word for that. And one of Madame Rondel's haughtiest and most trusted young ladies would always carry them back to Madame la Baronne's villa, on hangers, at arm's length, with never the smallest crease in the golden silk, and the starched collars and cuffs a gleaming white, literally gleaming, for one polished and polished them with a special iron till they positively glowed.

On rainy days, and praise be to kind heaven they weren't frequent, Madame Rondel would be as dignified as ever, but it would be crystal clear she simmered internally with fiendish ill-humour. All that elegant and fragile laundry had to be dried indoors instead of outside in the excellent sunshine. And woe betide any young lady who carelessly flicked her neat head against any of that dangling linen. So a rainy day would seem interminable, until suddenly, as if by magic, there would be Madame Rondel, majestically radiant, bowing and crying most joyously:

'Ah, bonjour, bonjour, Madame la Baronne!'

And there smiling at them all from the doorway would stand Madame la Baronne herself paying a friendly little visit to good Madame Rondel and her so-excellent Establishment.

'Bonjour, Madame Rondel,' would say that friendly lady.

Then all the young ladies would stand to smiling attention and chorus:

'Bonjour, Madame la Baronne!'

And she would give them the kindest of smiles and say:

'Bonjour, Mesdemoiselles!'

And Madame Rondel would say:

'It's been a long time since we had the pleasure of seeing Madame la Baronne.'

'Ah yes, indeed,' would reply Madame la Baronne in a tone of real regret. 'It hasn't rained for such a very long time! It seems an eternity since I last went out.'

Now this was the singular truth. Madame la Baronne meant it. She never did go out when the sun shone, only when it rained.

And this added to her golden lustre. One felt that only a great lady with ideas far above flat, stale custom would prefer the warm rain of Grasse to commonplace, everyday sunshine.

When late spring came, all the Mi-ladies including Madame la Baronne Alice de Rothschild, and the Mi-lords too, of course, began to leave sun-baked Grasse to avoid all the fatiguing summer sunshine. And just as everywhere else along the Côte d'Azur, the terraces of the fine expensive cafés and restaurants, the delightful villas and splendid hotels grew silent and deserted. And as Madame Rondel's clients, of course, were all among these distinguished winter and spring visitors, her Ironing Establishment, too, was closed for the summer season, and the services of her young ladies were no longer required. Madame Rondel would, of course, graciously re-engage them all towards the end of September.

This, however, was never a blow; everyone expected it, and promptly took up another job for the summer. Marie-Elisabeth herself always went to the Perfumery where her parents worked. Her summer job was to help carry around the all-important supplies of jasmine. Country women, arriving at dawn, would tip their loads of that sweet-smelling flower on the Perfumery floor, and Marie-Elisabeth would spend the live-long day packing baskets with jasmine, and then carry them around to this room or that, as required, two baskets at a time, one each side of a little wooden yoke across her shoulders for all the world like a milkmaid with her pails.

And heavens, how her shoulders, her arms, her back would

ache the first week or so, until she got into her jasmine-stride as one might say. And one can have too much of any one perfume, no matter how sweet. Roses are different. Each rose has its own subtle scent, but jasmine is always jasmine, one recognises it a mile away, and it would seem to Marie-Elisabeth that she herself became absolutely impregnated, positively radiated jasmine, even when she lay in bed of a night, no matter how she scrubbed herself all over with strong carbolic soap.

However, a job was a job; and Marie-Elisabeth may have been spoilt but she had her pride; and 'one was not rich' as her Maman so often said. Also as she grew older she gratefully realised how hard her Maman and Papa always worked, especially her Maman who would sit up late into the night making her pretty clothes; and always cooked such very good meals for Papa and Marie-Elisabeth. So don't tell Marie-Elisabeth only children are always detestably ungrateful. It simply is not true.

Then the Sundays of summer were especially delightful, for it was now that a family had a worth-while opportunity to set out very early and visit their relations and friends and spend a long chatty day with them, catching up on all the news and gossip.

Marie-Elisabeth's Maman and Papa had relations living down there in Antibes, but don't ask her to work out just who had married whom in the years gone by, but somewhere in the family were the Paolinos from Calabria; and as the Corporal, Francesco's Papa, always fiercely proclaimed: 'Once a Paolino, always a Paolino. Let no-one ever forget that.'

So sometimes on a Sunday in summer Marie-Elisabeth would go with her parents to visit these relations, including the newly-arrived Paolinos from Calabria. By this time, of course, the uncles, aunts and cousins had all found homes for themselves, and Papa the Corporal and Mamma Paolino

had managed to find an old house roomy enough to accom-
modate them and their seven children. But Papa the Corporal
was still the head of the entire family, let no-one forget that
either, he still represented the good God in the whole Paolino
family, so there were always some other dutiful Paolinos calling
in to greet Papa the Corporal and ask for advice, or seek
approval of this and that. And this, of course, made for splendid
and lively discussions with everyone voicing an opinion, and
Mamma too, of course, joining in as she slapped extra plates
and glasses on the table for all the visitors.

Marie-Elisabeth loved visiting Papa the Corporal and
Mamma Paolino. It was not only the spontaneous warmth of the
Paolino welcome, there was also something so special, indeed
palpitating is the only word she can think of, to describe Papa
the Corporal and Mamma Paolino and their seven children.
Something dramatic was always happening to one or the other
of them, and when related by Mamma Paolino with the
eloquent aid of all the other Paolinos, one listened entranced
as if sitting spellbound in some theatre.

Above all Marie-Elisabeth loved to hear the dramatic tale
of Francesco the Bankrupt, the ex-'Cordonnier, Maître Bottier',
and the iniquities of those defaulting clients of his, tripping
elegantly off in their unpaid-for, hand-sewn, cric-crac-ing shoes.

The noble grandeur of this bankruptcy deeply impressed
and moved Marie-Elisabeth, for, as Mamma Paolino passionately declared, this sinful world was indeed coming to something when a Paolino became a bankrupt because his work
was *too* good, because he was the shining soul of honesty like
all other Paolinos – or Papa the Corporal would flay the skins
off their backs – and because, being a Paolino, he had nobly
trusted those black-hearted, slippery ladies.

But ah, but wait a moment! Mamma Paolino was steadily
exacting the cash, franc by franc, from those defaulting women,

and franc by franc the leather merchants were being paid – and in full.

And Marie-Elisabeth would sit there imagining all this, and wishing she'd had the luck to have a pair of those exciting cric-crac-ing shoes; and presently everything about Francesco the Bankrupt began to have something very romantic and appealing to little Marie-Elisabeth.

But of all the infuriating bankrupts! As soon as he had greeted Marie-Elisabeth and her Papa and Maman, he would make his excuses, and hurry off to spend his long summer Sunday on the Cap among the roses he was growing there. And there would sit all the other Paolinos and her own parents talking away, only pausing to take breath, or presently to sit down to devour a dish of Mamma Paolino's marvellous 'pasta asciutta' cooked as only Mamma knew how; and there would sit Marie-Elisabeth in her prettiest dress, her hair beautifully arranged, and that exasperating Francesco hadn't even seemed to notice her in his hurry to get away to the Cap and his roses. And as Mamma Paolino would proudly say he would only be back when it was so dark one couldn't tell a rose from a nettle. Ah, mamma mia, what a worker, her 'piccolo, gracile' Francesco had become!

Then off Mamma Paolino would go again, proudly telling how Francesco was definitely making a good living now. He was sensibly growing other marketable flowers as well as roses: carnations, gladioli, anemones, all the colours of the rainbow, and sweet-scented freesias too, but only yellow freesias, that being the fashionable colour in freesias then. Indeed, no florist, it seemed, would say thank you for any other colour, not in freesias, no matter how delicate and charming.

As for the roses he grew, 'Veramente bello!' cried Mamma Paolino, always the loveliest of colours, the longest of stems, the freshest of blooms. He gave value for cash down, did their Francesco.

Say what you please, however, it soon becomes tedious for a girl in her prettiest dress, her hair beautifully arranged, to sit there just listening, with the most interesting of all the Paolinos promptly bolting off every Sunday without one backward glance, without ever once suggesting she might like to come along and see all these flowers, above all the roses, he was growing out there on the Cap. Ah, no, he was exasperating, Francesco Paolino, in spite of all the glamour of his noble bankruptcy.

Then came one Sunday Marie-Elisabeth will never forget. She had put on a lovely new white dress, it reached to her ankles, of course, for she was now a young lady of seventeen, but it was beautifully ironed and trimmed with the daintiest of finely pleated frills. And on her dark hair she wore a new hat she had made herself of plaited crepe paper. Yes, yes, paper. Paper hats were all the rage that summer on the Côte d'Azur. They didn't precisely wear well, these paper hats, of course. One shower of rain and they were sodden ruins. But what matter? One tossed them away and made another, also for next to nothing. However, Marie-Elisabeth offered up a special prayer that it wouldn't rain on that special Sunday, for on the crown of her new paper hat she had tacked a whole garden of delicious artificial flowers.

She looked a picture; all the Paolinos said so – except that infuriating Francesco. He wasn't even there that Sunday when Marie-Elisabeth and her Papa and Maman arrived. He had already flown off to the Cap.

There was, of course, the usual tumultuous welcome, the usual splendid conversation and at mid-day the usual magnificent great dish of Mamma Paolino's 'pasta asciutta'. But presently Marie-Elisabeth and one of Francesco's sisters,

Conchita, decided to go for a little stroll, but once they were safely outside in the street Marie-Elisabeth staggered Conchita by carelessly suggesting that they might stroll for a change to the Cap and take a look at Francesco's flowers.

'Strolll' screamed Conchita. 'But it's kilometres away!' and she looked pointedly at Marie-Elisabeth's pretty little shoes. 'And it's not even a road once one gets to the Cap – only a rough track through the forest. You'd never manage it!' She obviously considered Marie-Elisabeth far too dainty and coddled to tackle such a walk, and Marie-Elisabeth, very nettled, retorted, oh, couldn't she, and that she walked kilometres and kilometres a day in the Perfumery of Grasse *and* carrying two heavy loads of jasmine as well. She wasn't afraid of walking, *and* in shoes like these, too. So good-natured Conchita laughed and said well, they'd see; and they set off.

Now it *was* a long way and the little track Francesco had made through the forest of the Cap was indeed rough, but the sun shone and the air was full of the warm good smell of pine and fir, and talking and laughing, the two girls presently came to it – Francesco's flower garden.

'But . . . but . . . it's wonderful!' breathed Marie-Elisabeth.

There, in a clearing of the forest, grew the most beautiful roses and other flowers in long neat rows, as well tended as any in the gardens of Madame la Baronne Alice de Rothschild herself. But it wasn't only this. No, there was something most moving, most unexpected, suddenly to come across so well-loved a garden in the midst of this wild tangled forest.

Surely Francesco was the most courageous, the most artistic of men. He had created all this loveliness with his own two hands. And suddenly Marie-Elisabeth felt ashamed; she understood now why Francesco loved to spend his Sundays in this scented quiet place.

She stooped to admire one of the roses, a beautiful yellow

one. 'Look,' she cried to Conchita, 'you remember I told you about Madame la Baronne's silk blouses? Well, they are this colour, this very colour!'

It was only then they were aware of him, standing silently watching them in the shade of a tree – the elusive Francesco. And he had overheard all she had said, for he now came forward, smiling.

'Then Madame la Baronne has excellent taste,' he said. 'And just smell it!'

He took a knife from his pocket, opened it, and swiftly cut off one of those yellow roses and held it out to Marie-Elisabeth.

'A – ah!' sighed Marie-Elisabeth.

And that rose did indeed have a wonderful perfume, better than any of the thousands she had loved to smell at the Perfumery of Grasse.

'It would look nice on that dress,' said Francesco. 'I like your hat, too.'

And immediately Marie-Elisabeth's heart began to sing like a bird. Francesco had no need to say more; indeed, he didn't even try to say more; but his eyes told her that he not only liked her new white dress, her pretty paper hat, but that he liked her, too. Yes, he liked her.

As she liked him.

But naturally she wasn't going to permit him to see this, at least not immediately. No, indeed, not after the way he'd always pretended not to notice her.

She ungratefully wished, however, that good-natured Conchita was not there but miles away, so that she and Francesco might be alone, just the two of them for once, among all these flowers, these lovely roses.

But no, there was that imperceptive Conchita now saying yes, yes, the yellow roses were very nice but come along, do, it was getting late and Papa the Corporal would be sending out a search-party for them, and he'd be blazing mad if they weren't sitting there, forks at the ready, the split moment Mamma was ready to set on the table the 'ratatouille' she had prepared for their Sunday supper.

And Francesco guffawed and said he most certainly didn't advise them to outrage Papa the Corporal and insult Mamma's 'ratatouille'. So they said 'Au revoir' and began to hurry back along the rough track through the forest. But when they came to a sharp bend and turned to wave, didn't that impossible Francesco already have his back to them! Wasn't he already intent on something among his roses!

But Marie-Elisabeth, not in the least infuriated, laughed aloud. She was still remembering, would always remember, the look in his eyes when he gave her the lovely yellow rose now pinned on her pretty white dress.

And the way he had smiled at her. Above all, the way Francesco had smiled.

CHAPTER FIVE

Visit to Chamboeuf

Early one bright summer Sunday in 1908 savoury smells began to drift through the open windows and door of the living-room – which was also the kitchen too, of course – of that small farm in the quiet unremarkable village of Chamboeuf where Papa Meilland was born.

His mother had been bustling round since daybreak preparing a festive and most ample meal. That Sunday was to be a very special family occasion, all four of her children were coming home for the day. Yes, home, thought their mother. This was still home to them all, thank God. True, three of them now had homes of their own as well, all three suitably married and all three living at a sensible distance so that ruinous train-fares didn't devour too much of their hard-earned cash when they visited each other now and again – as they should, thought their mother, as they most definitely should. She didn't hold with families drifting far apart, gradually becoming strangers one to the other. She couldn't bear to think of this happening to her own four children.

She was also grateful all four of them found ways and means to visit her too so regularly – especially now their father, the poor man, was dead.

Ah well, he was at rest; freed for ever now from those bitter memories of that Franco-Prussian War and the siege of

87

starving Paris. Dear Heaven, this was 1908 now, so that in-
glorious war was all of thirty-eight years ago, but it had
always been so close, so menacing a spectre to her poor man.

Well, now he was at peace with the good God who understands us all, and she piously crossed herself; and then sharply
ordered herself not to be a selfish old woman moping like this
on so special and lovely a Sunday.

All the same, it was sad he couldn't be there to see his
four children and to enjoy the good meal she was preparing.
However, he must know how well she was managing to cope;
otherwise there would be no peace for him, the poor man. So
he *must* know, decided Antoine's mother.

Yes, given her health and strength, she would never have
to hold out her hand for charity to anyone, please God, not
even to her own four children, good as gold as they were, all
four of them.

But for pity's sake why go on thinking like this, to-day of all
days! This was to be a real red-letter occasion. Their Antoine
was to marry too; and to-day he was bringing his fiancée
home for the very first time to meet all the rest of his family.

Everyone in Chamboeuf was already saying what an excel-
lent match it would be, for Antoine was to marry Claudia
Dubreuil, his 'patron's' daughter, indeed his only child.
Antoine asked Claudia; and then very properly requested her
Papa and Maman's permission to marry their daughter.
And they had been enchanted to say yes.

And they might well be enchanted, decided Antoine's
mother, for Antoine would make an excellent husband for
any girl, clever, hard-working, and tall and handsome into the
bargain. And merry and kind-hearted as well. And it wasn't
only his mother who thought so; everyone liked Antoine.

Antoine's mother then decided, not for the first time, that
Antoine was also worth his weight in gold to his 'patron',

Visit to Chamboeuf

Monsieur Dubreuil, who seemed to think nothing of going off, carefree as one pleased, to conferences of rose-growers, here, there, and everywhere. Antoine loyally maintained that this was excellent; that a professional rose-grower ought to know what was happening in the world of roses outside his own gardens, that he ought to meet and discuss points of interest with other rose-growers.

Well, that was as it might be, thought Antoine's mother. Monsieur Dubreuil might, indeed, go merrily off to his conferences knowing he could leave all those rose-bushes, all those fruit trees, in Antoine's capable, conscientious care.

One should be fair, however. It seemed Claudia, too, was capable and conscientious. A wonderful girl, Antoine said, so very pleasant and obliging to the clients. And she kept all the accounts and correspondence in the best of order as well as working hard in the gardens when she wasn't cooking or doing the housework. She even found time, it seemed, to make all her own clothes.

Ah yes, from the start Antoine had spoken most warmly about Claudia Dubreuil, often saying how patient and kind she always was to her ailing mother. A poor-spirited woman, that one, uncharitably thought Antoine's mother. She herself could never imagine any woman leaving so much to her daughter, no matter how poorly she felt.

But it was as if Antoine sensed this, for he was forever saying that Claudia was so different, altogether different, a girl after his mother's own heart.

Well, that remained to be seen, darkly thought his mother. First love always wore rose-coloured spectacles, and she herself had her secret maternal misgivings about this unknown girl. After all, Claudia had always been an only child; she had never known the rough and tumble of other children about her, the give and take of real family life.

Visit to Chamboeuf

But Antoine insisted she had never been spoilt; that, on the contrary, her parents, to his mind, had always leaned far too heavily on her, especially her ailing mother. And it was nothing short of a miracle, said Antoine, that Claudia hadn't taken to moping too in that hushed inhospitable house. But she was always bright and cheerful, always brimming over with new ideas, so full of life, and above all, of courage. And unlike her mother she dearly loved to meet people, to talk and laugh. Everyone liked Claudia, everyone.

Maybe, thought Antoine's mother; but girls can change. They often did once they were safely married. And what if Claudia later on gradually took after her mother, eternally ailing, devouring pills by the boxful and swallowing endless bottles of patent medicines, refusing to go out, and, worst of all, obstinately and gently closing the doors, one after the other, on all Antoine's family and friends. That would be terrible, unbearable.

Ah well, no sense in worrying over all this again. To-day she would see this Claudia Dubreuil; to-day she would *know*. Something deep inside her assured her that she would take one long look at this girl and she would most surely know. And there was no shaking off this strange expectant feeling, this coming certainty.

So she resolutely set her mind on mixing the dough for the old-fashioned farmhouse apricot tart that Antoine and the other three had loved when they were children. She decided to use the same battered old brown dish, a real family-sized dish, the one she had so often set before them on a Sunday and they, all four of them, spoons in hand, eagerly waiting around this very table.

She took a knife and most dexterously, using her one good hand and the hook on the other, began to halve the ripe apricots she had picked that morning fresh from the tree, when something made her look up at the four 'Certificats d'Etudes', neatly framed and hanging side by side on the wall. And again it surged up in her, the same warm pride and joy. Claudia would be sure to notice them; everyone did. And never mind if those four grown-up children of hers *did* begin to laugh and protest, she would certainly say it again, even if it was for the thousandth time: there was not a family in all Chamboeuf or for miles around who could equal that array of certificates, no, not one, not even now in 1908.

At this very moment it seems that Antoine and Claudia were setting out from Lyons to catch the morning train to Chamboeuf, both in their Sunday best, but not looking in the least like two happy young lovers with a whole shining free Sunday before them.

'What on earth has come over us?' wondered Claudia. 'We were both looking forward so much to to-day; and here we are now walking along so stiff and silent one would think we were strangers.'

And it seems that Antoine suddenly blurted out, 'What's that?' as if desperate to say something, anything at all to break this unbearable silence.

'He knows very well what it is,' thought Claudia, looking down at the neat long parcel she was carrying.

But all she found to say was 'Oh . . . this? Just a few roses . . .'

'Good,' said Antoine.

Then they were silent again every step of the way to the station.

Any other time, thought Claudia, she would be eagerly telling Antoine how she had gone to early Mass and then picked these roses, choosing only the loveliest pale yellow and soft pink ones, Antoine having once told her these were his mother's favourite colours in roses. And she had made one of the most beautiful bouquets of her life before she carefully wrapped the stems in damp cottonwool and slipped the bouquet into the neat long bag she had made the evening before of several layers of soft paper.

Any other time she would have taken the pins from the top of the bag, made Antoine look inside to see how delicately the colour of one rose shaded into the other, and they would both have exclaimed at such fragrance, such loveliness.

Any other time that wonderful feeling would have then caught at both their hearts as it always did at moments such as this, when something told them that this was one of the dearest, the most beautiful things about their love for each other. And that it would always be like this, they would love each other and roses to the end of their lives, the one love so closely entwined with the other that there could be no separating one from the other, ever.

Yet, there they were now, on so lovely a summer morning, with a beautiful bouquet of roses, and catching that train to Chamboeuf without a word, a smile between them.

Why, a passer-by would imagine they had quarrelled; or were on their way to be put on trial. Yes, that was precisely this oppressive feeling – they both felt, and looked, as if they were about to be tried. They were so absurdly, so childishly apprehensive about this visit to Chamboeuf. Both she and Antoine hated the thought of any possible cloud on their happiness; they so wanted Antoine's whole family to approve, and like *her*, Claudia Dubreuil. Above all, his mother, his splendid, indomitable, terrifying mother. It was as simple as that. But how could she expect Antoine to admit as much?

They sat solemnly down side by side in the train, the bouquet on Claudia's lap. She looked down at her best long brown skirt, her new brown kid gloves, her new silk blouse. She looked again at her blouse and wished she'd had the sense to buy a more discreet colour, not this warm rose-pink. But she had thought it such a lovely colour the day she had bought the material to make a new blouse to wear on her very first visit to Chamboeuf. Now she dismally wondered if Antoine's practical mother might think it highly unsuitable, downright gaudy in fact. But she herself dearly loved glowing colours, full of life and warmth, golden-yellows, copper-golds and warm rose-pinks. The trouble was that these were the only colours that 'did' anything for her, that seemed to go with her cream skin, her dark eyes and hair.

And Claudia wished once more that she had been born a real blonde like her Maman with pretty fair hair, blue eyes, and a pink and white complexion. Then she, too, would have looked elegant, lady-like, in navy blue. A navy blue costume and a white blouse were always safe, and in good taste.

However, it was too late now to do anything about the way she was dressed. There she sat in her gaudy new rose-pink blouse with even a gaudy rose-pink ribbon to match on her new brown hat. She must look a sight; hideous, simply hideous.

Suddenly she could have burst into tears, sitting there feeling so ugly and atrociously dressed. And longing for comfort, she put one hand on Antoine's.

He immediately took it and held it in his own warm strong hand and smiled down on her.

'We'll soon be there,' he said.

And there they sat, silent again, but now hand in hand, all the rest of the fifty kilometres to Chamboeuf.

When they walked through the open door into the living-room of that small farm in Chamboeuf it seemed full of laughing talking Meillands, but at first Claudia only saw

Visit to Chamboeuf

Antoine's mother, tall, very neat, every hair in place, turning towards her, anxious eyes reading her face, her very heart.

Claudia was never to forget the warm smile that then lit up her lined face and how she cried, 'So you have come at last! But come in, my child, come in!' And she took Claudia in her arms and kissed her most warmly, and then turned to kiss her tall son; and as in some crowded happy dream, Claudia was being kissed and shaking hands with all her future brothers and sisters-in-law, with Antoine's mother issuing orders left and right so that presently there was a chair for everyone around the table and the bouquet was unpacked and set in a jug with everyone admiring it and Antoine's mother crying, ah yes, give her a yellow or a real pink rose every time and one could keep all the other colours. And couldn't one of these great idle fellows stop talking just for a moment and find the strength to pick up the bottle she'd now set on the table and pour them all out a little 'apéritif'. Not that they needed an 'apéritif' to put an edge to their appetites, she trusted, not with the good meal she had ready for them, everything done to a turn though she said so herself.

It seems it truly was a wonderful meal they had that Sunday; as Antoine had so often told Claudia his mother was a first-class cook. But it wasn't the meal that was such a revelation to Claudia, it was the atmosphere, the feeling in the very air of that small farmhouse. It was something she had never experienced before; it was like being in some kind homely tale in a book – the mother keeping a loving eye on everyone and everything, never seated long in her chair, always jumping up to set this or that on the table, piling their plates, and asking a thousand questions.

Everything was so different from all Claudia had ever known. Her own mother was always so silent, so ailing. If ever a knock came at the door, she would shrink back and whisper, almost resentfully, 'Now who can that be!' always so fearful of any break, any strange voice, that might shatter the quiet monotony.

And there they were now, nine of them, merrily talking away with never a headache between them; and just as Antoine's mother had set a tall family-sized coffee pot on the table and a knock came at the door, it was she again who was the first to jump to her feet, eagerly crying, 'Ah, come in! Come in, Monsieur le Curé, and meet Antoine's fiancée!' And another chair was found for Monsieur le Curé and Antoine's mother insisted he, too, had a cup of coffee with them and a little glass of her special liqueur, the one she made herself from the wild sloes that grew free as air in the hedges, so acid and sharp, and yet making, when one knew how, *and* took the trouble, so excellent a liqueur, far better for the digestion and liver than any of these fancy bottles of heaven only knew what that sold at such a ridiculous price in the shops.

And yes, this was a special occasion, to be sure, she told Monsieur le Curé. Just look at them now around the table, not four, but eight of them under her roof. Eight of them!

This, thought Claudia, is how a family, a home, a real home should be. This was how *their* home would be, hers and Antoine's. Then a sudden sharp feeling of guilt swept over her and she assured herself that no, no, of course she was not criticising her own delicate little Maman. She was so very frail, always felt so tired, so unwell. Truly she was to be pitied.

And how fortunate, how very fortunate she herself was, thought Claudia, to have a whole ready-made family-in-law, all so willing to accept her, and please God one day to love her as well.

Soon there she was helping Antoine's mother and his sisters and sister-in-law to wash up whilst Antoine led the other men out to inspect that year's Lord Pig and stroll round the farm. And presently Antoine's sister, Marie, asked if Claudia had made her lovely silk blouse, such a becoming colour and so beautifully tucked and embroidered down the front and on the cuffs. And Claudia, shining with delight to think she couldn't look so hideous after all, eagerly offered to bring the pattern next time and cut them all out blouses just like her own.

Then Claudia never could remember just how, but the talk gradually drifted from fashions in blouses to fashions in Christian names, or how Antoine's mother came to say she firmly believed in giving children the names of good saints, of course, but, nevertheless. names that also wore well as one might say. That was why she had had her own four children christened: Marie, Clothilde, Antoine and Galmier, though, mind you, she herself would never have thought of Galmier if Monsieur le Curé, the learned man, hadn't preached a splendid and instructive sermon one day, informing them all that they might think Saint Galmier was simply the name of their nearby small town with all those springs of health-restoring water, but there had once been a Saint Galmier, a poor and most humble servant of God, as good and pure as that spring-water. Moreover, he had lived in these very parts a thousand long years ago, earning his bread by making stout locks and keys. In short, a hard-working saint after Antoine's mother's own heart.

But for the life of her, Antoine's mother could never fathom what had come over her own mother, for though she'd had her christened a sensible Jeanne, maybe so as not to outrage Monsieur le Curé, she'd always called her Jenny and saw to it that everyone else called her Jenny as well.

Yes, Jenny, of all the outlandish names, that's what Antoine's mother had always been called. After some singer, somebody had once suggested. But her mother had never admitted this, maybe because her own Jenny had turned out to have a voice like a crow with the croup.

Everyone laughed, but Claudia eagerly said, oh yes, it was true; there had, indeed, been a singer called Jenny, Jenny Lind. And she told them all she had ever read about that famous prima donna, saying she knew it sounded like a fairy-tale, but it was true, every word.

Well, well, said Antoine's mother, one certainly did live and *learn*. And this naturally led to those four 'Certificats d'Etudes' hanging on the wall; and they, of course, led to memories of those struggling but happy days when Marie, Clothilde, Galmier and Antoine went clattering off in their wooden-soled boots to study in school until they were twelve, all four of them.

Then it was time to go, and Claudia noticed that Antoine's mother had a little parcel ready for each of her children, some of her own butter and cheese, and a few fine pears, with strict orders to leave them till next Thursday or Friday when they would be just right to eat.

There was also a parcel for Claudia to take home to her Maman with compliments from Antoine's mother, and a message to say she hoped Madame Dubreuil would soon feel well enough to spend a day in Chamboeuf too. She would be most welcome.

But all Claudia herself could manage to say as she kissed Antoine's mother was a lame:

'Thank you, thank you. It's been a lovely day. I can't tell you how lovely.'

But she knew instinctively that Antoine's mother understood what was in her heart for she kissed her again and said:

'For me, too. This great son of mine is a lucky fellow. Come again soon, child!'

Then she stood in the door waving to them till they were out of sight.

Antoine pulled his watch from his waistcoat pocket and looked at it.

'Just time,' he decided. 'We'll take a quick look at Madame Mivière's old house.'

He didn't explain but Claudia knew that this was his one regret in all that golden day. Kind Madame Mivière would never see Claudia; she was dead, someone else now lived in her house.

Fortunately, the new owners must also have been keen gardeners. It would have been heart-rending to see that garden, where Antoine had spent so many happy hours, looking neglected, unloved. But it was beautiful, a real sight to behold, especially the roses.

Fortunately, too, no-one seemed to be about either in the garden or in the house, so they were able to linger at the gate for a while and exclaim at the scarlet 'Jean Liabaud', the golden-yellow 'Duchesse de Ausstädt', and Antoine's favourite 'Rosa Noisettiana', the charming delicate rose Pierre-Joseph Redouté had painted, the one the Empress Josephine had loved best of all – or so good Madame Mivière had always liked to believe.

And truly, cried Claudia, those old roses were the most generous, the most faithful of friends, for there they were still blooming away in this lovely garden just as they had bloomed when Antoine was a boy; just as they had bloomed long years ago in Josephine's beloved gardens at Malmaison.

And to think, went on Claudia, that she herself had typed the address on the catalogues that went to this very house, the catalogues Madame Mivière had lent to Antoine. How strange to think it was good Madame Mivière and her love of roses and those catalogues that had finally brought Antoine into her life . . . for ever.

Visit to Chamboeuf

'Yes,' said Antoine. And then added, 'My mother, Madame Mivière . . . and now you. My mother is right. I am, indeed, a lucky fellow.'

Claudia slipped her hand in his, and they turned and walked on to the station in silence.

There was no need for more words. This had, indeed, been a golden day, one they were to remember all their lives. Antoine's family had taken Claudia to their hearts; and she was his dear love, and he was hers.

And this, vowed Claudia, her heart brimming over with happiness, was how it would be in the long years to come. Always, please God, always.

CHAPTER SIX

Mamma Paolino and High Finance

Very early every morning, down there in the little town of Antibes, Mamma Paolino would take her two outsize string bags and briskly set off to snap up the 'best buys' of the day at the market. But on the way she always slipped into church, made a low and most reverent genuflection to the Saviour of Mankind, who still has so much on His hands, and then knelt down to say her morning prayers.

Mamma Paolino would then piously but firmly give her daily reminders to her favourite saints, urging them to bear in mind she was counting on them to go on lending her a hand, all that day as well, with the affairs of the Paolino family.

Presently Mamma Paolino began to invest in a daily candle to light to these kindly and patient saints with an extra petition urging them to lend even more force and persuasion to her maternal tongue in the discussions that were now raging night after night around the Paolino table.

These discussions were becoming increasingly dramatic and momentous. Wild and improbable as it may sound, the Paolinos, led by Mamma with the admiring support of Papa the Corporal, were now giving their close and eloquent attention to matters of High Finance, yes, yes, 'I Ricconi!' as Papa the Corporal proudly put it.

Mamma Paolino and High Finance

That wild rough land on the nearby Cap d'Antibes was still going for a song, still literally dirt-cheap, everyone still considering, if they considered it at all, that one needed to be a poverty-stricken land-hungry Calabrian even to contemplate the endless hours of sweat and toil that would be required to fell all those trees, root up that veritable jungle of brambles and bushes before one could even see the colour of that dirt-cheap land beneath.

But, as Mamma Paolino darkly declared, one day, one fatal day, some shrewd land-speculator would begin to be curious, he would hear a word here, a mention there, about a Calabrian who was beginning to grow very fine roses and vegetables out there on the Cap. And this land-speculator would quietly begin to ask questions, and then take a trip himself to the Cap, and go prowling round until, oh, Dio mio! he would come across the flowering and profitable oasis their Francesco had sweated to create with his own two hands among all those trees.

And Mamma Paolino could positively behold that land-speculator, standing there, frozen in his tracks, giving a low whistle of surprise to observe the rows of beautiful rose-bushes, the anemones, the yellow freesias, and the fine vegetables Francesco was growing out there on the Cap.

Mamma would then draw a lurid picture of this land-speculator, whirling around and scurrying like a hare to some lawyer's office. But once there, he would cunningly assume a careless 'take it or leave it' attitude, and end up by buying the whole of the Cap as like as not, at some give-away price.

And Zoom! Instantly up and up would soar the cost to poor honest people who had been scraping and saving for years to buy some of that once so dirt-cheap land.

Therefore, said Mamma, the moment had arrived! They, the Paolinos, must forestall any such land speculator and forthwith manage to buy a great slice of the land of the solitary, still un-discovered Cap.

Yes, yes, but with what, groaned Papa the Corporal and all the other Paolinos. Toil, sweat, scrape, save as they might, never wasting a crust, a sou, and every shirt, every dress, on their backs mass-produced by Mamma herself with never a centimetre of material, a bone button wasted, how could there ever be enough in Mamma's purse to put down the money for that land.

Not for years and years, maybe never, not with the wages for which all Calabrians, no matter how intelligent and industrious, were expected to toil most gratefully.

But Papa the Corporal and those other doubting Paolinos were reckoning without Mamma, backed, of course, to her mind, by those faithful saints. Clever Mamma Paolino had come a long, long way since they arrived in Antibes a few short years ago with next to nothing in the family purse. Not only had she so speedily learnt to haggle fluently – in French of a sort – so that they were all most amply well-fed at a minimum cost, but shrewd Mamma Paolino had also realised that it was, indeed, most unlikely that they would ever be able to save enough money to pay cash-down for a worth-while stretch of that dirt-cheap land. So Mamma, if you please, had been conducting her own investigation into the astute and money-making ways of 'I Ricconi' – High Finance.

And Mamma had discovered that there were moneyed people about who never did a stroke of real work themselves but sat back and let their money work for them. And that these financiers were always looking around for ways and means of making their money work ever more profitably, but still with the minimum of bother or risk to themselves, of course.

Mamma Paolino and High Finance

These financiers, said Mamma, were therefore always prepared to lend money to reliable, honest, industrious people, from whom they could collect a good steady interest with the comfortable assurance that their money was as safe as in a bank, indeed safer than in some banks their knowledgeable Mamma could now mention.

And were not the Paolinos, cried Mamma, now known to be reliable, honest, industrious . . . but why go on with the litany? All they had to do now was look round for one of these financiers. And having found him, no naïve taking him along to see Francesco's garden. No, indeed, they, too, had to be hard-headed. They would take him to some wild stretch of the Cap, and say that this was what they *might* be prepared to buy, this wilderness, but only at a wilderness price, of course.

And then leave the rest to their Mamma, and her favourite saints.

One evening Mamma Paolino set a pot of extra-strong coffee on the table, poured them all out a fortifying half-cup, and dropped her bomb.

She had discovered the very financier. He, too, had naturally made his searching inquiries; and doubtlessly impressed by all he had gathered, he was prepared to lend the reliable, honest, industrious Paolino family enough ready money to buy a fine large slice of the land on the Cap.

Mamma Paolino then took a deep breath, and added:

'At twenty per cent.'

Twenty per cent, bellowed Papa the Corporal and the other Paolinos. Daylight robbery! A Calabrian brigand would be the soul of sweet charity compared with Mamma's financier! Saints in heaven, they would have to kill themselves to pay that interest alone. Or had Mamma taken leave of her senses! Hadn't she realised they would all have to go on with their usual jobs for a long, long while, and slave away every spare moment as well as to clear that land before they could even grow a row of cabbages upon it.

Mamma retorted that honest sweat and toil had never yet killed any Paolino; and that she had, of course, consulted the highest possible authority – Heaven itself. She had offered a solemn Novena to Our Lady of Good Counsel, and what had happened? Not only had that financier turned up out of the blue, fallen from heaven as one might say; but she herself now felt, right here, in her innermost heart, that the moment had arrived to borrow that money, yes, yes, even at twenty per cent. They *must* buy that land – Presto!

And tell her, just tell her, cried Mamma now flaming with wounded dignity, had she ever permitted any one of her family to starve, walk around in rags? Had she not always worn out her brains, her fingers to the very bone, to find ways and means to feed and clothe them all, and save something too for *their* future? And did they now mean to sit there and pierce her to the very heart imagining that she, their Mamma, was cold-bloodedly prepared to behold them slaving away, year in, year out, eternally paying that twenty per cent interest, world without end, amen, amen!

Ah no, what kind of a poor imbecile did they take their Mamma to be!

Having reduced them all to penitent silence for a moment, Mamma, with considerable hauteur, then informed them that she had given most careful attention to their first step, 'le premier pas qui coûte' as the French put it. And this first critical step that counted was to engage an excellent lawyer, one who could conduct business in both French and Italian; Mamma had enough cash in her purse to pay his fee. And they would instruct this bilingual lawyer to draw up a cast-iron contract in both languages for that loan; and this cast-iron contract would most clearly and emphatically state in both languages that they, the Paolinos, could pay back all this loan at any moment, any hour of any day they felt so inclined.

That did it! Papa the Corporal and all the Paolinos positively exploded again until Mamma shouted them down, crying no, she did NOT expect a shining miracle with banknotes falling like manna from heaven. And NO, she was not expecting to win the princely 'Gros Lot' of the National Lottery. All she expected was a little intelligent silence when she, their Mamma, had something of vital importance to tell them.

So there was silence again. And Mamma solemnly said:

'Union makes strength.'

She trusted even her thick-headed family agreed on this. Very well then, they would all pull together, work longer and harder than ever before, and all the while she, Mamma Paolino, would continue her tireless investigations; and presently, as sure as the sun shone in the sky, she would discover a second financier who would say, well, in view of all he had heard of the safe, reliable, honest, industrious Paolinos, he would be prepared to lend the money to pay back that first financier, but . . . but . . .

Mamma Paolino, like all great orators, knew the value of suspense, so she paused and let them all sit there, waiting.

And then added:

'But . . . at fifteen per cent!'

And again, Presto, subito! they would borrow enough of this fifteen-per-cent money to pay back the twenty-per-cent financier. And with no legal quibbling whatever, thanks to that clause in their cast-iron contract.

Much encouraged by this saving of five per cent, they would all toil away with even greater enthusiasm; and presently their indefatigable Mamma would unearth a third financier who, much impressed by the qualities, the monetary stability of the hard-working Paolinos, would be only too happy to advance them a loan – at ten per cent.

And again Presto, subito! they would borrow enough of this still cheaper money to pay back the fifteen-per-cent financier.

And so it would continue, declared Mamma Paolino, as confident as the Director of the Bank of France himself, the interest on that loan would go down and down, and finally, with one tremendous heave-ho, they would pay back every franc of the loan itself to the very last of all financiers.

And on that glorious victorious day, all that fine great slice of land on the Cap would belong to them, the Paolinos; and their Papa the Corporal and Mamma could sit back, wipe the sweat from their aged brows, and leave the family to get on with it. They, their parents, would have done their duty: they could die in peace.

The splendid audacity of Mamma's plan, and above all her blazing belief in heaven, and in them, swept them all off their feet; and to cram a momentous financial deal in a nutshell, the Paolinos borrowed enough money, at twenty per cent, to buy a large stretch of the wild rough land of the Cap.

And truly it was wonderful to see how Mamma's faith in heaven and in her family worked the miracle, for the Paolinos, who had arrived in Antibes with nothing but their high courage, worked every hour of daylight, never sparing themselves; and slowly but steadily whittled down the interest on that borrowed money and began to repay the loan, every one of them participating in each financial move with passionate pride.

And slowly but steadily they began to clear the wilderness they had bought and began to dig and plant that solitary place. And Mamma's heart brimmed over with joy and gratitude to heaven, to behold that wilderness begin to 'blossom as the rose'.

Mamma Paolino and High Finance

Moreover, when her older sons married, their young wives were swept straight into that close-knit family, straight into the Paolino Plan for the future. And Mamma's new daughters-in-law meekly wore Mamma's identical mass-produced dresses, meekly worked as long and hard as all the other Paolinos. True, this was fully expected of them, but they, too, learned to love, respect and, admit it, fear Papa the Corporal and Mamma Paolino. But in that order, definitely that order: love first.

Even now, after all these years, ask any one of them and you will be told that this was how it was: one could not help loving, respecting, and fearing Papa the Corporal, the head of the tribe; and above all, one loved Mamma; one dearly loved Mamma.

All this while Francesco, too, of course, was working away from dawn to dusk on the Cap, steadily paying for his own stretch of land, and steadily making an excellent reputation for himself with his beautiful dawn-cut roses, his long-stemmed gay anemones, his yellow freesias and his fine carnations, not to mention his impeccable asparagus and cauliflowers, and tender green peas and young beans.

But it was still roses that Francesco loved dearest of all. It was still his dream to grow only roses one day, nothing but roses.

Then, as Mamma Paolino often said, their Francesco might not have grown much, but he was now strong and healthy as an ox, for which Mamma piously gave grateful thanks to her favourite saints, of course, who had so conscientiously protected her 'gracile piccolo' Francesco from the perils of exposure to all that fresh air and sunshine out there on the Cap.

And now there was their strong, healthy and successful Francesco vigorously exercising his rights to argue and thresh out family affairs as vehemently as any other Paolino; and yet turning a deaf ear or muttering an exasperated 'Questo proprio no!', 'Why the hurry!' when Mamma began to say he was well over twenty now and it was high time he too began to look around for a good strong sensible wife.

You must understand that a respectable Calabrian family takes marriage very seriously indeed. Everyone in the family would be outraged, mortally offended, if a son or daughter rushed headlong into marriage without as much as a dutiful by-your-leave. Everyone expects to be notified, consulted, so that they may all have the pleasure of discussing, advising, exhorting and finally approving. But there was their infuriating Francesco showing no interest whatever, never once suggesting a suitable bride for himself, a good daughter-in-law for his Mamma and Papa the Corporal.

'Too busy,' he always declared, and would promptly pull on his boots and get back to his roses.

Very well then, since Francesco was too wrapped up in his roses, it would have to be the high duty, and pleasure, of Mamma and the rest of the family to fix him up with the ideal wife. Some strong, strapping girl, they decided, as amiable as she was hard-working, a girl used to working long hours out on the land, a willing, pious good girl, who would pull her weight with all the other Paolinos.

And, said someone, some saint of a girl who wouldn't mind taking second place to roses.

His loving family did even more than draw up the necessary qualifications for the ideal wife for their dilatory Francesco. They themselves began to bring this and that unattached and suitable girl to his attention. But that ungrateful Francesco would listen in silence and then turn them down, every strong pious strapping one.

Then came the day when Mamma Paolino demanded to know if he realised he was now getting on for twenty-eight.

Mamma Paolino and High Finance

Twenty-eight! And still unmarried. And what in the devil was he waiting for? Some angel straight from heaven?

Heaven forbid, said Francesco, but as they were all so determined to marry him off, he might as well say he'd had a girl in mind for years but he'd also had his pride. He had resolved to wait until he could offer her a reasonable future. But now things were going well, he would do as they so ardently desired, and ask this girl to marry him. And wait, wait, before they all began to roar at him! They would most certainly approve, for they already knew this girl and indeed were already very fond of her. And before they could get their breath back, he announced she was pretty little Marie-Elisabeth Greco, the daughter of their distant cousin of Grasse.

It seems that Mamma and the others just stared at him, at first not believing their ears. And then began to chorus, as expected, that of course they were fond of little Marie-Elisabeth, but consider, in the name of commonsense, consider how small and dainty she was, always dressed like a little princess. Could anyone picture Marie-Elisabeth working by Francesco's side out there on the Cap? No, one could not.

And she couldn't even cook. Her own Maman freely admitted as much. She was an only child, so pretty and dainty a child that both her Maman and Papa, though far from rich, had always loved to spoil her.

They agreed that little Marie-Elisabeth certainly did work long hours in her Perfumery and her Ironing Establishment, but that was sheltered lady-like work; and once she arrived home her Maman never permitted her to lift a finger; she was waited on like a little queen.

Francesco, face as black as a thundercloud, let them talk themselves hoarse, then maybe Mamma Paolino recognized the same look in his eyes she had seen that day he had told her he had decided to spend his life growing roses. And half-laughing, half-weeping, she began to say, well, they certainly did know, and already loved little Marie-Elisabeth. And she supposed this explained why Marie-Elisabeth too had been worrying her poor Maman to death for the last few years, turning up her pretty little nose at one suitable, love-sick young man after another, so that her Maman had been driven to declare that, pretty as she was, if she didn't stop being so difficult her Marie-Elisabeth might well end up going through life a solitary spinster. And to think all the while . . .

Mamma couldn't finish the sentence. She began to laugh till her sides shook. So did all the other Paolinos. To think, as someone declared, how blind a family could be; or was it how deep these two astonishing lovers had been, never letting a soul suspect they were in love?

But wait a moment! Had Francesco ever consulted Marie-Elisabeth about becoming a Paolino? Or had he been too busy even for that?

Francesco retorted that there had been no need. Marie-Elisabeth and he had understood one another from the start, but that he was thinking of going to Grasse that very Sunday to have a talk with her Papa and Maman. And Marie-Elisabeth too, of course.

And this explains, in a nutshell, how on January 10th, 1911, pretty dainty little Marie-Elisabeth Greco married Rose-grower Francesco Giacomo Paolino in Antibes, Antibes being more convenient for everyone than Grasse. And it may be well over fifty years ago now, but little Marie-Elisabeth still chuckles and wipes away a sentimental tear to remember her splendid, her wonderful wedding-day.

Every possible Paolino, by birth or marriage, turned up, of course, man, woman and child, well over fifty of them. And then there were any number of friends, and florists and old faithful customers. And they all made a beautiful long festive day of it, with a splendid wedding-luncheon, *and* a dinner at night, with a two-page printed menu for every one of them. Marie-Elisabeth can still show you that well-planned menu, though she still can't think what came over her to choose the picture on the cover, a poetical but most unwedding-like picture of a Grecian lady standing on a marble terrace gracefully casting bread to two stately swans on a romantic lake. But everyone else thought it lovely too; and, indeed, the whole day went off like a happy, gay, crowded dream. The wedding-luncheon from the Hors-d'Oeuvre Variés to the Champagne le Roy was a real banquet. Then those Paolinos with golden Italian voices sang song after song like angels; and they all danced, and the hours whisked by, and believe it or not, down they all sat again that evening to another veritable banquet.

And the next day they were all back at work again.

Now like all young couples, Marie-Elisabeth and Francesco dreamed of a home, a house all their own one day. And theirs, of course, they decided, would be out there on the Cap with the windows looking out on the rose-gardens. But now they had to be sensible, practical, and save very hard. So Marie-Elisabeth too became one of Mamma Paolino's meek young daughters-in-law. Presently she, too, found herself wearing one of Mamma's identical, mass-produced dresses, hating to hurt Mamma's feelings by even complaining, or wincing.

Then, at first, as everyone expected, Marie-Elisabeth stayed home. She simply would not have been any help out there on the Cap, not even at weeding. She knew, and the Paolinos knew, that she couldn't recognise freesia seedlings from chickweed. So in a noble blaze of wifely duty she offered to take on the cooking – *all* the cooking.

She also hotly declared that, of course, she knew how to make a good 'pasta asciutta', the Paolinos' favourite dish.

Hadn't she watched her own Maman and Mamma Paolino make it a thousand times and more?

But alas, as all young wives soon discover, it is one thing to watch one's own mother or mother-in-law toss off a dish fit to set before a king – or the Paolinos – and quite another to tackle it, solo. And old as she is now, Marie-Elisabeth still vividly recalls the first 'pasta asciutta' she set before the ravenous Paolinos with her brand-new husband beaming away, also expecting wonders.

First of all, as tradition demands, she served up the 'pasta', a vast steaming dish of tender 'pasta' smothered with a rich meat sauce. And 'mamma mia'! It was marvellous, that sauce! Only Mamma Paolino seemed most unnaturally reserved, even silent. Could it be professional jealousy?

No, it was not. All was explained when Marie-Elisabeth set the traditional second course on the table, a great dish of the meat. Now economy and good Italian sense demand that one first gently stews the meat to make the rich sauce to smother the 'pasta', but one must take infinite care so that it not only supplies that rich sauce but it, the meat, as well, is also a feast in itself, still deliciously juicy and tender.

And the moment she set that satanic meat on the table, Marie-Elisabeth's jubilant heart sank into her buttoned boots. It looked terrible. And it *was* terrible, so dry and stringy, all the goodness, the flavour, the juices, mopped up by that magnificent extravagant sauce.

Mamma Paolino, bless her great heart, at once began to find excuses and to rattle off directions and warnings to prevent a second disaster. But those other Paolinos, including her brand-new husband, guffawed like lunatics when someone set his plateful of stringy meat down on the floor for Perla, the Paolino dog, and that detestable animal sniffed it and walked off, her nose in the air. Oh, a fine Paolino joke that was; and still is to this very day.

And Marie-Elisabeth may have cried herself to sleep that night, but she soon showed those guffawing Paolinos! She determinedly set to work to learn to cook just like Mamma Paolino; and to-day her 'pasta asciutta' is famous among all friends and relations. I myself can swear to that.

But this wasn't the only surprise in store for the Paolinos. Marie-Elisabeth decided she, too, could learn to recognise a weed when she saw one; and she began to get up at crack of dawn and trudge all the way to the Cap with Francesco. She, too, was going to do her share of work on the land; to be honest, she was also secretly bored to tears staying home alone all day doing the family cooking.

But heavens, the cooking, or carrying round baskets of jasmine, or standing ironing all day, seemed delightful child's play compared to that weeding! Those weeds on the Cap grew by the millions, or at least they seemed millions upon millions to her. But Marie-Elisabeth wasn't going to be beaten, not by weeds, and she doggedly weeded on, back aching infernally, and at first often impatiently tugging up many an innocent seedling, mistaking them for weeds, and then stuffing them back into the earth again, praying no sharp-eyed Paolino had spotted her mistake so that her weeding too would become a fine Paolino joke.

But she learned, oh yes, Marie-Elisabeth soon learned; and to do far more than weeding, too. A girl doesn't need the bulging muscles of a prize-fighter to become an accomplished gardener.

And a girl doesn't need to be born a poet to be strangely moved to arrive in a garden set in a forest, the day still sparkling new, the sun shining in the morning sky, and all the birds singing. Say what one likes, there is something about a garden at dawn, above all a rose garden, something most lovely, almost holy.

Not that she and Francesco could afford to stand idle long. The bunches of roses had to be on the market-place of Antibes, or on the train heading for Nice, long, long before the distinguished visitors in their villas and hotels were pulling the bell-ropes for the pots of tea they always swallowed before they rose from their beds, or so everyone said.

So up and down between the rows of rose-bushes they would both go, and soon Francesco was trusting Marie-Elisabeth to work alone, cutting and bunching roses as deftly as he did. Marie-Elisabeth had not learned to iron the most fragile and lovely tea-gowns and blouses for nothing. She, too, knew how to use her eyes, her hands.

She knew even more. She had been to school until she was twelve and even if she had dodged all the more tedious lessons that demanded eyesight like an eagle's, she, at least, knew how to read and write. And Francesco did not. He, of course, had never gone to school. But now he decided he must learn, above all, to read; and that Marie-Elisabeth must teach him.

So day after day when the sun stood high in the sky over the Cap, and their appetites, too, told them it was time to eat, they would sit down in the shade, their backs against a tree, and have a picnic-meal. Then out would come Francesco's first reading-primer – a newspaper. And even now Marie-Elisabeth still marvels at the speed with which Francesco learned to recognise letters, capitals and small, figures, and then words. She had always known he was clever, quick-witted, but now he staggered her. He was brilliant, her Francesco. If only *he* had had the chance to go to school, he'd have beaten everyone, come out top of his class every time. And soon there he was, buying an evening newspaper, and reading aloud the headlines about the latest in crimes,

and football results, and the antics of politicians; or as he himself put it, getting his money's worth and educating the
family as well, reluctant as most of them were to shut up
and listen to him.

But the newspaper headlines were only the spring-board as
it were. Soon Francesco was hard at work studying, mastering, something that it seemed he had always longed to read.
It was a rose-catalogue, a very different publication from the
artistic catalogues of to-day. There were no illustrations
whatever, only neat lists of the roses offered for sale, each
one most soberly described in the fewest possible words,
followed by the price. And all in such tiny, economical print
that, as Marie-Elisabeth exclaimed, one had indeed to long
to read it, to be a real rose-lover, to be tempted to study it
at all – it looked so dull.

But little did they dream how strange and poignant it would
seem in the years to come to remember that the rose-catalogue,
which Francesco now studied with Marie-Elisabeth's help,
came from a professional rose-grower with many excellent
new roses of his own to his credit, a certain Monsieur Francis
Dubreuil, with gardens on the outskirts of Lyons.

Yes, Francis Dubreuil himself, Claudia's father, who had
once regularly sent catalogues to good Madame Mivière of
Chamboeuf.

And who now began to send his catalogues, by request,
to a new and most discerning customer:

> Monsieur F. Paolino,
> Rose-grower,
> Cap d'Antibes,
> Alpes Maritimes.

CHAPTER SEVEN

War to End All Wars

Up there in Lyons there had also been a wedding. That other young rose-grower, Antoine Meilland, was now also a married man. On December 4th, 1909, he had married Claudia—Claudia Dubreuil, of course, his 'patron's' daughter.

It was on this occasion that Claudia's mother positively staggered them all. For years she had been the most retiring, the quietest of semi-invalids, yet now she insisted on the very grandest wedding: cabs drawn by white horses, coachmen with white bows on their whips, Claudia looking radiant and absolutely Parisian in a lovely white wedding-dress, her Maman looking ethereal but also absolutely Parisian in a gown of exquisite black lace, and the bridegroom himself feeling, and doubtlessly looking, exquisitely uncomfortable in full evening dress. Yes, yes, full evening dress as worn by English gentlemen to balls and banquets at Buckingham Palace – this gentlemanly rig-out being considered 'de rigueur' for all French bridegrooms at high-class weddings.

The wedding-reception too had to be very grand and formal in one of the finest restaurants on the finest square in Lyons, some say the finest square in Europe – the stately Place Bellecour.

But the excellent food and wine, and no doubt the shining happiness of the young couple, quickly thawed all ceremonious formality. And soon everyone was talking and laughing, and all those with good voices were easily persuaded to stand up and give them a song; and this easy conviviality presently made the bridegroom forget his high stiff white collar, he only knew he was the happiest man on earth, even if he was disguised as an English nobleman; and he remembers throwing back his head and singing the choruses with the best. In short, in spite of all the splendour, everything went off most happily.

And the next day, just like that other unknown rose-grower and his young wife down on the Cap d'Antibes, Antoine and Claudia, too, were both back at work again.

For them, however, there was one lovely difference – they had their own little home. They had found a small flat very near the rose-gardens so Antoine hadn't far to cycle to work, and Claudia could put in a few hours every day doing everything possible for her delicate mother.

But they had their own small home – to themselves. And they wouldn't have changed it for any palace on earth.

Now there were, of course, the usual knowledgeable busybodies who decided that theirs was another of these hardheaded, one-eye-on-business marriages, the up-and-coming employé sensibly marrying his 'patron's' daughter. And it was certainly true that Francis Dubreuil, Claudia's father, was now very well-known, and not only for the excellence of the rose-bushes and young fruit-trees he grew and sold; he was also widely recognised to be an expert and gifted hybridist, who had put some delightful new roses of his own on the market, 'Sarah Bernhardt', for instance. But in those days a hybridist who created any new variety of plant or flower earned plenty of esteem, but precious little in hard cash, even for some beautiful new variety that captured everyone's fancy and sold by the thousand, a variety that may have taken him years and years of patient work to create and perfect.

Hybridists were not then protected by any laws of patent. Anyone, for instance, was free as air to buy a few dozen or so bushes of some completely new and beautiful rose, and from these, if he was skilled at 'budding', he could produce and sell as many as 10,000 bushes of that new rose within a year. And never pay a penny more, never send a postcard to say thank you to the man who might well have taken long years to create it.

And the sober truth was that Francis Dubreuil, like his own father-in-law, Joseph Rambaux before him, was rich only in his love of roses.

So, too, were Antoine and Claudia, rich only in their love of roses, and rich beyond words in their love one for the other. And when a year later a little son arrived, they decided no-one could possibly be happier than they were; and they looked and looked at him and naturally thought he must be the most beautiful baby in France, and they named him Francis after his grandfather, Francis Dubreuil. And brand-new Papa Antoine Meilland, remembering good Madame Mivière, solemnly promised heaven to have the patience to teach his own child to use the eyes the good God had given him so that he too might always know the joy of seeing for himself the wonder and beauty, not only of roses, but of all the forests and fields, the whole world around him.

As for Antoine's mother, her pride in her grandson was lovely and touching to see, and from the moment he could speak, little Francis called her Grand'mère Jenny. But don't ask anyone why. Nobody even recalls telling him that his granny had been called Jenny when she was a child. All any-one can tell you is that Francis decided she was his Grand'mère Jenny; and that soon everyone forgot she had any other name, and she became Grand'mère Jenny to one and all.

War to End All Wars

It was just about this time too that friends and neighbours passing by and seeing Antoine at work began to give a jocular shout of 'Bonjour, Papa Meilland!' And maybe it was the wide smile the brand-new Papa would give them, but soon there he was, Papa Meilland, to one and all. And that is how he is called to this very day. He is still Papa Meilland to everyone, everywhere.

Claudia, of course, was now busier than ever with her little son, their own small home, still keeping the accounts, seeing to all the correspondence and never missing a day without running in to do this and that for her delicate mother. And when she had a free moment she dearly loved to lend a hand with the roses, singing away and thinking that the world had never been so kind, so wonderful.

Maybe this was why she so passionately believed the newspapers were exaggerating, of course, just being sensational, when they began to come out with more and more stories of heel-clicking German officers who were now, by imperial order, addressing their Kaiser as: 'My All-Highest War Lord'.

'My All-Highest War Lord!' As in some comic opera, decided Claudia. No, it simply couldn't be taken seriously. It just couldn't be true.

Down there on the Cap d'Antibes, life also shone kind and full of promise for that other young rose-grower and his dainty little wife.

Their slice of land on the Cap was paid for at last, and now that longed-for small house was being built there. For over three years Marie-Elisabeth had been imagining, planning, that little house. The windows were to look over the rose-gardens, of course, and on the side looking down to the sea, there was going to be a wide terrace, shaded with a vine, where they could sit and eat in the cool of an evening when the day's work was done.

And on this terrace Marie-Elisabeth was going to have a long table, a very long table so as to be able to seat Papa the Corporal and Mamma Paolino and Francesco's sisters and sisters-in-law, his brothers and brothers-in-law – the whole Paolino family.

All seven of Papa the Corporal and Mamma Paolino's children were married now, and thanks to their own skill, their own hard work, and, of course, Mamma's genius for High Finance, they were all doing very well, a real credit to proud Papa the Corporal and Mamma Paolino.

Well, there around that very long table on the terrace before that small house on the Cap would sit all these clever, successful Paolinos by birth or marriage, when Marie-Elisabeth graciously invited them to come and spend a long Sunday with her and Francesco in their new house on the Cap. But first, of course, she would take them on a tour of inspection, all around the beautifully kept gardens, not a weed anywhere, then all round the spotless house, and then insist on them all sitting down around that long table to drink a little apéritif whilst she, politely but firmly declining all offers of help, would dash back to her kitchen.

Then out from the kitchen she would come, magnificently carrying a superb 'pasta asciutta' and set that down before the admiring Paolinos; and this would be followed by a regal dish of meat, fit to set before Queen Victoria, the Baroness Alice de Rothschild, Mamma Paolino and yes, that detestable dog, Perla.

Oh, once in their own little house now being built on the Cap, Marie-Elisabeth was going to blow sky-high, and for ever, all last lingering Paolino doubts that Francesco would have done far better for himself by marrying some meek, brawny girl with bulging muscles – even if he did wince every daybreak at the sight of her.

All this, of course, was half a century ago now, but Marie-Elisabeth still chuckles to remember how she planned to prove most dramatically that an only child, spoilt and adored by her Papa and Maman, could turn out as good and hard-working a wife as any stalwart girl hand-picked by the Paolinos.

But to be serious, when she looks back now on those first years of their married life, she realises how much they taught her, above all, how much she learned from Mamma Paolino – and not only to cook. Any girl can learn to cook from a book, but to live with Mamma Paolino was to learn first hand the hard way, but the good, generous way to live as one of a large family.

Indeed, Marie-Elisabeth now considers that Mamma Paolino was a saint among women, a splendid authoritative saint, with an edge to her tongue when required, but with a great heart brimming over with love for them all, most un-selfish love and devotion.

But Marie-Elisabeth won't put on the rose-tinted spectacles of old age and sentimentality and most untruthfully declare she never once had a mis-word, a flaming quarrel, a good grizzle in all the years she lived as part of the Paolino family. She most certainly did. In fact, she regularly went into most ungrateful secret huddles with Madeleine, the wife of Francesco's brother, Nicolas. Together these two young Paolino daughters-in-law would let off steam, especially about the tyranny of being made to feel they, too, ought to be most grateful and wear – never daring to complain – those dull, frightful dresses mass-produced so regularly by Mamma Paolino, and presented to them by Mamma, with Papa the Corporal and all the other male Paolinos applauding as if they were the latest creations from Paris.

In fact, Marie-Elisabeth also put in a lot of hard thought about how best and most tactfully she could dodge Mamma's dresses once she and Francesco were at last blissfully living in their small house out on the Cap. Once there, she decided, she would begin to buy 'Le Petit Echo de la Mode' and send away for paper patterns, even wear spectacles on her nose, and begin to turn out the most ravishing of dresses – with Francesco's critical advice, of course.

You must understand that Marie-Elisabeth was forever being astonished by Francesco. To her mind he could also easily have made a great 'couturier' up there in Paris like Paquin and Worth. He would take one look at her when the new Paolino dresses were issued, and decisively, without a moment's hesitation, secretly direct her to take a tuck here or there, or lift up the sleeve a little here at the shoulder, so that with all these minor corrections, even one of Mamma's dresses would take on a small something extra, almost a 'chic', that made all the comforting difference. But she had to make all these alterations when Mamma was safely out of the way, of course. No Paolino daughter or daughter-in-law ever had the nerve, the heart, to wipe the triumphant satisfaction from Mamma's face when like Paquin and Worth, she presented her 'Paolino Collection' – all identical models, of course, in various sizes.

But none of this was really important. What truly began to worry Marie-Elisabeth was that there was no sign of a baby – especially as all the other newly-married Paolinos were busily presenting proud Mamma and Papa the Corporal with the most handsome and bouncing of grandchildren.

Then she would try to comfort herself, thinking that once they were in their own little home out there on the Cap, then surely she and Francesco would get their heart's desire. And the sentimental tears would come to Marie-Elisabeth's eyes to picture the rip-roaring Paolino welcome their first baby would have with Mamma weeping like a joyous fountain and rocking it against her warm generous bosom crying, 'Oh, vieni pezzettino mio! Oh, bambino mio!'

But this was the year 1914, and alas for the dreams, the hopes, the plans of so many millions of people the world over, that 'All-Highest War Lord', Kaiser Wilhelm of Germany, had no eyes, no ears, no thought for babies, grannies, roses, or any other kind and homely thing, only for cannons, guns, and clock-work goose-stepping armies. And one heartlessly lovely day up there near Lyons, young Papa Meilland received his 'calling up' papers, kissed his little family, took a long, long look at his roses, his young fruit trees, and marched off to fight for France.

Down there at Antibes, however, it seems that the military authorities were positively wincing to note down the unheroic height and weight of Rose-grower Francesco Paolino. But they optimistically slapped a tape-measure around his chest and commanded him to breathe in; allez! allez! deeper than *that* if he pleased. But breathe in as he might till he felt he would take off like a balloon, that unheroic chest of his still fell centimetres short of the expanse of chest demanded of a recruit if he was to have the honour and glory of fighting for the Republic of France.

'Too small,' they decided, just as his Mamma had once done.

But then they discovered that he had once been a 'Cordonnier, Maître Boittier' and promptly drafted him into the 'Service Auxiliaire' – behind the lines.

And believe it or not, but 'behind the lines' for Private Paolino turned out to be Nice, yes, yes, the nearby sunny city of Nice on the blue Mediterranean. And they fitted him up with tools and a safe, sheltered workshop and set him to work exercising his trained cobbler's eye checking Army boots to be sent to the men at the Front.

And Army boots it was for Private Paolino, nothing but boots, boots, boots, all through the months, the years, of that First World War – the one they swore 'was to end all wars'. So Private Paolino said 'Amen to that!' and patriotically got down to those boots.

Mamma mia! Those boots! He beheld them even in his sleep, regiment upon regiment of Army boots marching relentlessly left-right – left-right the whole night through.

But don't pity Private Paolino too much. In fact, don't pity him at all. From the military point of view, Nice might have been 'behind the lines', but it was still no distance at all from the Cap d'Antibes. And many a time did Private Paolino cadge a lift in a lorry and roar off to the Cap to lend a hand to little Marie-Elisabeth, who with sleeves forever rolled up, was toiling non-stop, day in, day out, to keep their garden going. But now peas, beans, cauliflowers, cabbages, tomatoes, onions and potatoes grew where once the yellow freesias, anemones and many another lovely scented flower had bloomed. Indeed, on all that land there was now only a selected few of their finest rose-bushes; they would need those bushes to begin all over again once this war was over and won.

But now France had great need of vegetables; so vegetables it was for little Marie-Elisabeth all through the months, the years, of that war. However, there was one solid comfort – the roof was now safely on their small house on the Cap. It had gone on the very day war broke out. So though nothing was as joyous as Marie-Elisabeth had dreamed, she and Francesco had their small house, a roof over their heads; and realised, none better, that they were far, far more fortunate than so many millions of others. And realising this, they soberly got on with it, Marie-Elisabeth with the vegetables, and Francesco with those boots.

As for Papa the Corporal, he too toiled on the land, and nightly held forth, explaining to Mamma how the Allies could finish off this war at the double if they'd only listen to men like him, men with seven years' hard experience in the Army. But Mamma working all day too, of course, wished the Kaiser at the bottom of the deep blue sea, and thought only of the Paolinos by birth or by marriage, both those fighting for France and those on the Italian front. And every morning when she knelt in church she now piously but firmly reminded her favourite saints to see to it that all those satanic bullets whistled high over their heads, and that they all came safely back to their wives and families.

And call it miracle, or just Paolino good luck or what you will, but when that war was over, every fighting Paolino came home to hug and kiss Papa the Corporal, Mamma, and his rejoicing wife and children. And so, too, of course, did that sheltered 'piccolo, gracile' military cobbler of the family – Private Paolino. But, of course, everyone expected that. So no medals, no laurel wreaths came his way, for who remembers the boots – if they were comfortable – once an Army has done with marching.

But ex-Private Paolino rejoiced with the others; and straightaway gratefully got down to re-planning his garden; and now that the war 'to end all wars' was won, he decided with Marie-Elisabeth to devote almost all their land to roses, with just a prudent side-line or two of other first-class flowers and prime vegetables.

Little Francis Meilland up there near Lyons was only five when this First World War broke out, but he, too, was to remember those war-years all his life long.

Papa was away at the war so it was Maman who had to see to the fruit trees, and dig and plant the garden, growing vegetables where once Papa's roses had grown. No one now, explained Maman, had the time or money to buy and plant rose-bushes, but everyone needed good vegetables and fruit.

However, Maman kept one part of the garden still planted with some of Papa's best-selling roses: Gloire de Dijon, for instance, which Maman said was one of the best-natured roses in the world, never demanding to be spoilt but obligingly growing anywhere in a garden or climbing up a wall, north, south, east or west. And Maman would point out what lovely buds it had, saying these made up for the fully blown blooms which were rather homely and flat, but one simply forgets that on a hot summer day, for those flat homely roses had a most delicious old-fashioned scent. And little Francis would stand and sniff one, and solemnly agree.

When the war was won, Papa would need these 'Gloire de Dijon' and those bushes of other best-selling roses to start a rose-garden all over again. But now, till Papa came back from helping to win the war . . . whatever that was . . . Maman had to grow and sell vegetables, and the fruit from the trees in the orchard, too, of course.

Then Maman also had to take care of her own mother, his Grand'mère Dubreuil. His Grandfather Dubreuil was now dead, and Grand'mère Dubreuil had come to live with them. But she was far too delicate to help Maman; and Francis also had a feeling she found him tiresome and noisy, always expecting him to remember to keep very quiet or he'd bring on one of her terrible headaches.

Very early every morning Francis and Maman would get up and steal down the stairs like mice so as not to wake up Grand'mère Dubreuil; and set off to market, trying to get there before the clock struck five so they could sell their vegetables as early as possible – there was always so much for Maman to do when they came home. And Francis would try his hardest to help push Maman's heavy hand-cart piled high with vegetables along the three kilometres of country roads to the Quai Saint Antoine, the very same market where Maman had loved to sell bunches of beautiful roses when she was a girl.

But now there was no faithful old Bichette trit-trotting gaily along, pulling a little cart bright with baskets of roses. No, there was only this heavy hand-cart laden with vegetables, but Maman would sturdily and cheerfully push it along, with Francis trotting beside her helping to push; and as they went she would tell him again all about Bichette and what a good friend she had been, and how she used to sing to Bichette as they trotted along and tell her stories.

Maman would always talk to Francis as if he were grown-up, telling him about Papa who would surely come marching home one day when he'd helped the Generals to win the war; and they would begin growing roses again; yes, Francis too would have his own little garden. And Papa would do more than grow and sell rose-bushes and young fruit trees, he, too, would begin to marry one rose to another and give the world some beautiful new roses just as Francis's grandpapa Dubreuil had done, and his great-grandpapa Joseph Rambaux before him.

And yes, to be sure, just as he, Francis Meilland, would do when he grew up. Papa would teach him.

This, of course, would lead to stories about good Madame Mivière who had taught Papa so much when he was a boy, and talking away, they would at last arrive at the Quai Saint Antoine, take up their place, and begin to sell their vegetables and any fruit in season.

Presently Francis began to do more than just help to push that heavy hand-cart. He decided to help to earn some money as well, and he would pick the chickweed that grew wild and free on the fringe of the road, tie it into neat little bunches, pile them, too, on the hand-cart, and push away with all his might.

Then, feeling very proud and every inch a man, he would stand by Maman's side and offer his bunches of chickweed to ladies with canaries singing away in cages at home. And these sympathetic ladies would pat his head and pay him two sous a bunch. This made him feel a real help, especially on cold or rainy mornings when the hand-cart seemed heavier than ever to push along those three kilometres of lonely roads.

Maman always tried to sell her vegetables as quickly as possible, though she never permitted even the chattiest of customers to see what a hurry they were in. She always had a smile, a friendly word for everyone, patiently turning over the cabbages or cauliflowers till she found just the size a customer wanted; but as soon as the vegetables were sold, away they would go, pushing along the empty hand-cart.

The moment they got in, Maman would hurry around preparing a little light meal for Grand'mère Dubreuil up in her quiet room, who had no appetite at all and had to be tempted to eat to keep up her strength. And all the while the good thick vegetable soup Maman had made the evening before, would be heating up on the stove, and when it was piping hot Francis and Maman would sit down and enjoy a great plateful.

Then came the moment of triumph for little Francis. He would count the sous he had earned with his bunches of chickweed and drop them one by one into a special money-box; and Maman would say just wait, all this money would come in very useful one day.

Then, like children the world over, Francis loved to hear the same story again and again, and this was the moment when Maman would tell how Papa too had saved his sous when he was a boy, one by one, till he had thirty of them; and how he went to Saint Etienne one day with Grand'mère Jenny and bought his very first budding-knife, the best knife he ever had, and bought with his very own savings.

In short, little Francis Meilland saw his mother courageously working every hour of the day all through that war and it always filled him with emotion to remember how joyous she made it all seem, how patient and kind she was to her ailing mother, never once losing heart, at least, never before Francis, as if she knew how important it is for a child to feel safe, confident, and quite certain that his Papa would come home again when the war was won, and everything would be just as it used to be.

He was also to remember how his mother courageously decided to make herself a pair of trousers. Today, it seems plain commonsense for a woman doing a man's job out on the land in all winds and weather to wear trousers. But in those days of long skirts to the ankle, the very idea was considered outrageous, unwomanly, almost indecent; and Claudia Meilland was certainly the first woman in that part of France to have the moral courage, the initiative to decide that long skirts and white petticoats flapping about one's ankles were ridiculous and infuriating. So she designed and made herself trousers, and wore them as she worked in the garden and orchard.

Then, busy and hard-up as she most certainly was, Claudia found the money and the time to take little Francis now and again to spend a Sunday with Grand'mère Jenny at Chamboeuf.

Francis loved these Sundays, not only because of the train-ride, but because he and Grand'mère Jenny were the very best of friends. He could chatter away to her and never once give her a headache. On the contrary she enjoyed their conversations every bit as much as he did. And Grand'mère

Jenny would have a lovely meal ready for them, and for one long blessed day, Claudia would be forbidden to lift a finger, and she could come home refreshed, rested, ready to tackle life again. Ah yes, Grand'mère Jenny was always the best of tonics.

But the best moments of all in these five long war years were the days when the postman would bring a letter addressed to:

Madame A. Meilland.

It would be a letter from Papa, of course, and to little Francis the words: 'Madame A. Meilland' shone like gold. They meant his mother, and that was how those words shone in his heart all his life long.

And to Private A. Meilland in the trenches of Flanders, 'Madame A. Meilland' meant the dearest, the most courageous of wives.

In 1919, Private A. Meilland was demobilised and came home to his wife and little son; and at crack of dawn the following day he was out looking at the few favourite rose-bushes in that one corner of the garden, still in excellent shape, thanks to heaven and Claudia. And he confidently told himself that from now on, with 'the war to end all wars' over and won, surely the world had learned to recognise the futility, the idiocy of hatred between nations and the madness of wholesale slaughter. Now he could peacefully get on with growing his roses his whole life long.

But one cannot wave a wand and all is restored, not even in a rose-garden. Before Papa Meilland could even begin to think of 'budding', propagating their small collection of best-selling roses, he needed 'understock', the hardy wild rose-bushes into which he must insert the living bud, the 'eye' as some growers call it, of these chosen roses.

Now there are certain nursery-men who specialise in supplying this hardy 'understock' to professional rose-growers. But many thousands of these had been called up to fight in the war, and those who had come safely home, also had to begin all over again, digging over their land, planting the wild rose seeds, waiting for them to grow into bushes. All of which takes time, of course.

Meanwhile, up and up soared the price of any available 'understock' still on the market, together with the cost of everything else one needed; and as the prices went up, down and down sank the value of all one's hard-earned savings.

So that first year Papa Meilland would disappear at dawn with his spade tied on his bicycle and come cycling back with the heaviest possible load of young wild-roses that he himself had found and dug up in the nearby forest.

But he knew he couldn't possibly go on finding and digging up his own 'understock' in this way. It was far too time-wasting and therefore costly. Not only this, but these wild roses he found in the forest could only be used to create tall standard roses. For bush roses he definitely needed dwarf 'understock' which he hadn't the time, or ground, to grow himself from seed, and which he couldn't afford to buy from the men who specialised in nothing but that.

However, he had made a start. He was at least able to 'bud' those wild forest roses, and so create and sell a modest number of good standard rose-trees.

The following year they scraped together enough ready money to buy twenty thousand dwarf 'understock', telling each other the price was exorbitant but that they must now make a *real* start no matter what the cost. And Papa Meilland still recalls their pride when Claudia and he surveyed those twenty thousand bushes all expertly budded, the first Meilland collection to offer to their clients.

With hope soaring high he and Claudia then sat down to compose the catalogue for that first post-war collection, with a foreword to all esteemed clients saying that one deeply regretted to inform them that Monsieur Francis Dubreuil was dead; but that the business had been taken over by his son-in-law and associate, Antoine Meilland, also an expert and experienced rose-grower, who now pledged himself to continue to merit the esteem and patronage of all Monsieur Francis Dubreuil's former clients.

But those catalogues were never sent out. All that expensive first collection of roses was devastated, wiped out before their eyes by a vicious plague of beetle, the Americans call it 'May Bug'. This atrocious 'May Bug' lays eggs from which hatch big white worms that literally devour the roots of roses. And there was nothing, simply nothing they could do to save those costly, all important bushes. The insecticides that now protect rose-bushes from the 'May Bug' and other deadly pests were not known in those days. And one cruel day they had to tackle the heart-breaking job of setting fire, burning to ashes, all that fine first collection, every single bush, knowing all the while that next year, somehow, some way, they must manage to find the money to buy a second stock of that costly 'understock'. And begin all over again.

And many, many a time did Papa Meilland thank God he had listened to good Madame Mivière and gone off, all unwilling as he was, to work among trees as Claudia's father had suggested in that first long-ago letter. For now he was at least able to work hard and long in the orchard, and propagate and sell excellent young fruit trees, and so keep the wolf from galloping straight through the door.

The third year, however, all went well, and at last Rose-grower Antoine Meilland was ready to send out his catalogue and that carefully composed foreword. And he well remembers one cold, rainswept evening when Claudia was briskly typing the names and addresses on the wrappers for these catalogues, she came to a sudden halt when she came to the name and address of one client who before the war had at first bought a very modest number of her father's roses, but had then regularly increased his yearly order.

'Must be heavenly down there,' she sighed. 'Think of it! The blue sea, orange and lemon trees, palms and mimosa, and such glorious sunshine. And people who sit and talk to one at the drop of a hat, as if they'd known one all their lives.'

There was something in her voice that made Papa Meilland go over to her, and when he looked, he saw she had just typed:

> Monsieur Francesco Paolino,
> Rose-grower,
> Cap d'Antibes,
> Alpes Maritimes.

'We'll save up and go there one day for a holiday,' she said. 'It's the one place I've always longed to see.'

Then she laughed as if she was joking, of course. People with their modest income could never afford to take a real holiday, apart from a day or two off now and again. They didn't even expect to, not in those days.

And for many a long year Papa Meilland was never to give this another thought, for the simple reason that Claudia herself also seemed to forget all about it.

Down there on the sunny Cap d'Antibes, Rose-grower Francesco Paolino sat on his terrace before his house and carefully read the foreword and then studied the contents of this new Meilland catalogue; and decided to give this unknown Antoine Meilland a chance. But if his bushes didn't come up to the high standards of his papa-in-law, Francis Dubreuil, then ps . . . ss . . .stl away would fly this esteemed client.

Rose-grower Paolino also grandly informed his interested wife that he proposed taking a trip to Lyons one day and inspecting the Meilland rose-gardens. One might easily pick up a profitable tip or two.

Splendid, said his wife, but he would, of course, have to go alone. She couldn't possibly spare the time now to go round with him inspecting other people's rose-gardens and picking up tips. No, not now. Her place was here, at home.

And there by her side slept the reason – in a cradle. That longed-for baby had at last arrived, a beautiful little girl, Louisette.

CHAPTER EIGHT

Tassin

It was then in those difficult years immediately after the First World War, that the city of Lyons seemed to give a great heave and begin to grow, reaching out and swallowing up the green countryside about it as it grew.

In the days of Joseph Rambaux and his son-in-law, Francis Dubreuil, their orchard of fruit trees, their rose-gardens, their little house had been in the quiet outskirts of the city, but now all about them, factories were beginning to spring up like mushrooms and tall chimneys began to belch black smoke where once birds chattered and sang among the orchards, green fields and hedges.

By 1923, only four short years after Papa Meilland was demobilised, it was becoming clearer and clearer that much as they hated the thought of it, a move would have to be made; and the sooner the better before the price of land in a quieter, more favourable spot for rose-growing, soared even higher. And to cut short much heart-searching, Papa Meilland and Claudia most reluctantly and regretfully decided to sell the house, garden and orchard so full of memories for them both and with the proceeds buy a modest house and four acres of land at Tassin, a tranquil rural district some five kilometres to the west of Lyons. Claudia's mother, as always, left everything to them, plaintively agreeing with

Claudia that better air and more quiet would be good for her, too.

It was then, too, that Papa Meilland had to summon up all his courage to make the hardest, the harshest decision of his life. He must face cold reality: abandon all dreams of creating new roses of his own one day. He had not worked long years with Claudia's father, Francis Dubreuil, for nothing. He knew, none better, the time-absorbing patience, the long years of endless work one needed to create and perfect any new rose. And as the English saying goes: 'Time is money.' For many, many a year, he would need every hour, every franc, to improve those four acres of land, restock their new gardens, and get the business going.

It seems Papa Meilland then resolutely counted his blessings – always a salutary exercise at times like this. He was his own master; he was doing work he dearly loved – and one cannot say as much for so many millions of others; and he had the best of wives and a lively, most intelligent small son.

Very well then, since he couldn't create new roses of his own, he would grow the best and most beautiful of the roses already on the market, sell only the finest of bushes guaranteed to give lasting pleasure and satisfaction to all who bought them. And he rolled up his sleeves and got down to those four acres of land; and presently they most literally 'blossomed as the rose', and many a warm summer evening, he would stand there at dusk, caught up in the same wonder and delight he had known as a child in good Madame Mivière's garden. And then turn, to see Claudia by his side, sharing all his unspoken thoughts. For a moment they would stand there, silent; then she would give a little laugh, tug at his sleeves and say for pity's sake, supper was ready, growing cold on the table.

The older he grows, the more Papa Meilland realises how much, how very much he owed to his wife, Claudia. He could go out of a morning, get down to work among his roses, whistling away with so quiet and easy a mind. Claudia tackled all the correspondence, the sending out of catalogues, the paying of taxes, all of which Papa Meilland heartily detested; she also kept their home so clean and orderly and far better still, so comfortable, so friendly a place where everyone was always made to feel welcome. She made all her own clothes; and until he was old enough to leave their local Primary School and go to a Lycée in Lyons, she made everything for Francis as well. And she most patiently and lovingly cared for her ailing mother still closeted among her patent medicines and pills in her own quiet room, engrossed only in her own bad health.

And the miracle was, that with all this on her clever capable hands, she still found time to help in the garden, and when the roses were in bloom, she took the warmest delight in cutting them at dawn, making beautiful bunches of them that were eagerly bought by clients who often turned up to inspect the bushes in bloom before they decided to send in their next order.

And there was something so warm about Claudia; she brought such a joyous zest to everything she tackled, and this, of course, made all the difference to life. They worked long and hard but life was always good, kind, and sane, and never, never dull – not with Claudia.

Papa Meilland can still see them, for instance, setting out after Mass on a Sunday, merrily bowling along on their battered bicycles, he, Claudia and Francis, leaving everything behind for the day including his gentle, ailing mother-in-law – in charge of someone kind and patient, Claudia would see to that.

Away they would pedal, free as air, into the foothills of the nearby Cevennes, singing, whistling, talking as they sped along.

There were no traffic-jams on the roads in those days, no 'bumper to bonnet' queues of hooting motorists; they often met no-one at all for kilometres and kilometres. Then they'd choose some lonely spot, leave their cycles there under some bushes, and wander away for hours on end through the quiet forest. There is always so much to see and learn in a forest; and Papa Meilland, remembering good Madame Mivière, delighted to point out this and that to his own small son. He was, for instance, thanks to Madame Mivière, quite an expert on where to look for edible mushrooms – he also enjoys eating them. And soon Francis, too, was learning just where to look, and how to recognise the different kinds. But what did that lad do, but set to work to out-do his Papa. He began to borrow books from a free library in Lyons, and before he was twelve he was calling them by all their Latin names, which as his Papa would say, made even the most delicious of mushrooms sound ominously indigestible, in fact, positively poisonous if one hadn't already eaten whole platefuls of them over the years and still lived to pick more.

Towards Christmas and the New Year they would tramp for hours searching for holly and mistletoe and an evergreen that Papa Meilland himself had always dismissed as 'petit houx' – 'little holly'. He and the other lads of Chamboeuf had always called it this when they went out gathering ever-greens to decorate the 'crèche' in church at Christmas. But now his botanical son borrowed more library books and pored over them until he found the correct name for this festive little bush with its deep green leaves and gay scarlet berries. It was ruscus, he informed his Papa: ruscus.

But it was his Papa who taught his erudite son the correct, the kind way to cut branches of this ruscus and all other living bushes and trees so that one never harmed or mutilated them in any way. Then back home they would pedal, with ravenous appetites, and bundles of mistletoe, holly and ruscus tied on their bicycles. And after supper, Claudia loved to arrange all this into gay, appealing bunches which the florists of Lyons were only too pleased to buy on the Monday.

Now, for all their hard work, and Claudia's careful and most intelligent management, they always had to be careful and thrifty, but they decided that Francis should have the money earned with these festive bunches to save with his 'bunches-of-chickweed-money'. And his Maman would always say:

'You'll see! It will all come in useful one day.'

Then Papa Meilland encouraged his son to plant peach stones in his own little plot of land – just to see what would happen. And the Emperor Napoleon reviewing the Imperial Guard, could not have been prouder than young Francis Meilland when he reviewed his first squadron of tiny peach trees.

Then, always remembering Madame Mivière, Papa Meilland patiently taught him how to transplant them, handling them with care and intelligence, never overcrowding them, but leaving them the right, but not extravagant, room to grow; and later on, most wonderful of all to Francis, his father taught him to 'bud' and propagate them just as he himself had learned to do in Saint Galmier. And the money earned with the sale of these young peach trees also went into Francis's savings-book to swell the chickweed, holly, mistletoe and ruscus accounts. And again his Maman would say:

'You'll see! It will all come in useful one day.'

But far, far more useful than any savings, of course, was the ideal way Francis was always encouraged and taught to use more and more expertly the eyes and hands the good God had given him. Papa Meilland was keeping the solemn promise he had made to heaven when he saw his son, lying there, in his cradle.

Now, in France, as you may already know, school-children have a holiday not on Saturday, but on Thursday. And like his Papa before him, Francis found life outside school far more interesting than sitting nailed to a desk in a classroom. But believe Papa Meilland, Francis was never at any time made to feel he ought to be dutiful, lend a hand on a Thursday with the roses. No, definitely no.

But every Thursday, on would go a well-loved old pair of blue drill trousers, and there he would be, eagerly learning to do this job and that. And later on in life, he wrote:

'Thursday was always the happiest day of the week for me. I was free to work among roses.'

And what else could one expect, says Papa Meilland. It ran in the lad's blood from both sides of the family.

Then, until he was twelve, Francis had always easily come out top of his class – much to their pride and pleasure. So naturally, Papa Meilland and Claudia planned to give him the best possible education, let him continue his studies at his Lycée in Lyons until he was crowned with that glittering French certificate of higher education: the 'Baccalauréat' known to all irreverent French youth as the 'Bacchot' or even more briefly the 'Bac'.

But to their disappointment and dismay, once he was twelve, Francis showed no desire whatever to be crowned with the 'Bacchot'. Indeed, he showed no concern at all when his marks slumped down to rock-bottom; and for the next two years, he begged, pleaded and entreated them to let him leave the Lycée, and begin his real life's work, the only work he wanted to do – out there in the rose-gardens.

Tassin

He said he'd had enough of books, and deaf to all exhortations to show a little sense, if he pleased, to behave with more intelligence, he obstinately dug in his young heels, and stared idly through the windows, the despair of all the exasperated 'Messieurs les Professeurs' of the Lycée of Lyons, not to mention Papa Meilland and Claudia, too, of course.

In the end they gave in. One cannot stuff further education down a boy's unwilling throat as if he were some unhappy goose in Dordogne; and on July 14th, 1926, Francis Meilland, aged fourteen, solemnly put on the new jacket and trousers of his first real gardener's outfit – in France this is always made of stiff, stout blue drill – and sat down to the first breakfast of his working life.

And the tears came to Claudia's eyes to see how solemnly he then followed his Papa, similarly clad, into the gardens: Antoine Meilland and Son, Rose-growers.

It was a blazing day, that fourteenth of July, and up there in Paris, and five kilometres away in Lyons, and in every other town and village of France, including Chamboeuf, brass bands were playing away, Messieurs the Mayors in their red, white and blue mayoral sashes were making fine resounding speeches bringing in the Fall of the Bastille, the defeat of Tyranny, and the glorious birth of Liberty, Fraternity and Equality; and then doubtlessly sitting down to patriotic banquets and raising many a patriotic glass to the Republic of France.

But in those four acres at Tassin one couldn't afford to take a patriotic day off – there was urgent work to be done. This was the time for budding, inserting the living bud of the rose to be propagated into the dwarf 'understock' – in a cut one makes close to the ground in that part of each hardy young wild rose where the stem ceases to be green and the roots begin.

Tassin

A back-aching and skilled job, for once inserted, each bud must promptly be tied securely into place. And to speed things up, Papa Meilland now employed an experienced old hand who followed close on his heels, binding each bud safely in place as swiftly and expertly as Papa Meilland inserted them. It was to be his son's first job to give a little help to this experienced old hand.

But fourteen-year-old Francis decided to do more than give a little amateur help. He had obviously made up his mind to prove he could work every bit as fast and well as that experienced old hand. Maybe what he really wanted to demonstrate was how right he had been to insist on leaving the Lycée all uncrowned as he was by that glittering 'Baccalauréat', since this was where he so clearly belonged, this was where all his aptitudes lay, here among roses. And the proof? Behold him now taking to his vocation in life as easily and naturally as a duck to water.

Papa Meilland says the sun blazed in the cloudless sky, the sweat ran down their faces, but Francis grimly kept close on their experienced heels, never wasting a moment. His back, his legs, must have ached infernally but when Papa Meilland charitably asked, well, what about it, perhaps he'd had enough for his very first day, Francis wiped the sweat from his brow and haughtily said certainly not, he was as fresh as a daisy, and to prove it he worked on even more doggedly, tying in buds for dear life as if his whole future reputation depended upon keeping pace with that experienced old hand.

Then this, too, still makes Papa Meilland chuckle. When at his Lycée in Lyons, Francis had never shown the slightest interest in learning English. But one day an English gentleman called on them and fortunately he knew some French, for the little English Francis had bothered to acquire would have gone into a match-box. However, between them it was established that this quietly-spoken gentleman was an horti-culturist; and it naturally pleased Papa Meilland to learn that he had been recommended to visit the Meilland rose-gardens whilst he was in France. So they took him around and Papa Meilland could see that Francis was mentally kicking himself for not knowing more English, that he would dearly have loved to talk to this well-informed English horticulturist, who had not only heard about the Meilland rose-gardens, he also knew all about the ten new roses created by Joseph Rambaux, his great-grandfather, and the sixty-four created by his grandfather, Francis Dubreuil.

And here was Francis Meilland, their unworthy descendant, idiotically tongue-tied, when he ought to have been able to converse in English with this interesting visitor, answer him, and ask him questions as well.

But that did it, says Papa Meilland. Francis promptly decided to make up for the hours he had squandered, staring through the Lycée windows when he should have been mastering the language of Shakespeare and Charles Dickens; and he at once joined an evening-class in Lyons and began to study English Language and Literature.

Now this meant leaving home immediately after supper and cycling five kilometres to Lyons, so he could hardly expect to be home again before eleven o'clock on these evenings. Yet not only did Francis cycle off to those classes as regular as clockwork, but on the evenings when there was no class, there would sit their anti-'Bacchot' of a son, his head deep in his books, muttering away, mastering English Language and Literature, the most exemplary and assiduous of students.

But it was the evening Francis went off to his very first evening-class that was later to become so significant to Papa Meilland. Francis had wished them both good night, told them on no account to sit up for him, and said yes, look, he *did* have his keys, and then as he was hurrying through the door, he suddenly turned to look at them.

'Do you know,' he said, 'I now think that one day I shall travel round the world.'

And he was serious, absolutely serious. He meant it.

Papa Meilland remembers laughing and saying that Francis Jules Verne Meilland had better make a start then by travelling safely back from Lyons in the dark. But it seems Claudia looked at her son, and smiled, the gravest of smiles, as if she saw nothing at all amazing in this fantastic remark. And years later Papa Meilland was often to recall that strange moment, his son standing there in the doorway, so eager, so young, and his mother smiling at him as if silently agreeing:

'But of course! Why not?'

Now as his father-in-law, Francis Dubreuil, had done, Papa Meilland always tried to manage to find the time to attend the more important meetings and conferences of professional rose-growers. This was very pleasant, as well as plain common-sense. It gave them all a chance to exchange views and ideas, take part in many a profitable professional argument, and also to meet old friends, and make new ones. In fact, Claudia used to say it was well worth the train fare just to listen to all he had to tell them when he came home from one of these meetings.

When Francis was seventeen, Papa Meilland returned from a meeting one night and announced he'd received the most interesting and unusual invitation from a certain Monsieur Mallerin.

Now Monsieur Mallerin was very well known and liked in the rose-growing world. He'd once had an excellent job with a prosperous company in Grenoble that specialised in central heating. At that time roses had just been an absorbing hobby of his. He not only loved to grow them in his garden at home but he also liked to try an amateur hand at cross-pollinating one rose with another. As the years went by, however, Monsieur Mallerin began to realise that his heart was set more and more on roses, and less and less on central heating. And he was fortunate, he was comfortably off, so he decided to abandon radiators and boilers and settle down to do as he pleased for the rest of his life. And he bought himself a charming little estate at Varce, some twelve kilometres from Grenoble and there he lived most contentedly among his fruit trees, his vegetable-garden, his bee-hives, his chicken-houses, and best loved of all, of course, his roses. Moreover, maybe to his own surprise, he made an excellent living selling the produce of all this, or as Papa Meilland puts it, he became a successful French edition of an English 'gentleman-farmer'.

Far more delightful to Monsieur Mallerin, however, was the success he now began to have with his cross-pollination. He not only created some lovely new roses, he also budded and propagated them, and placed them on the market. In short, he became a successful professional 'gentleman-rose-grower' as well.

Now, after this particular meeting, Monsieur Mallerin had cordially invited a few rose-growers to spend a day soon with him at Varce. There was nothing unusual in this, Monsieur Mallerin was very hospitable, but this *was* strange; on this occasion he invited only those rose-growers who had a son old enough to take an intelligent and affectionate interest in roses, and asked these fathers to be sure and bring their rose-loving sons with them to Varce as well. He said he had just created a rose that he thought might well interest these fathers and their up-and-coming sons.

So one lovely summer day in 1929, there they were, that band of rose-growers and their sons, strolling in the sunshine around Monsieur Mallerin's charming estate in Varce; and Monsieur Mallerin certainly didn't go in for segregation of any kind. It was enchanting, for instance, to come across beds of roses blooming happily but most unexpectedly among his fruit trees, or bee-hives.

Presently, he led them to a little row of young rose-bushes – the new variety he had just created. They were just coming into full bloom, a most beautiful golden yellow, and there were forty petals to each rose, so Monsieur Mallerin said. The foliage too was delightful, a rich soft glowing green.

Later on, Monsieur Mallerin budded and propagated this lovely new yellow rose and put it on the market under the name of 'Madame Pierre S. Du Pont'; and to his amazement the Americans fell head over heels in love with 'Madame Pierre S. Du Pont', and bought thousands of bushes to plant in their gardens.

But now there it bloomed on that summer day, unknown to all the world outside that little estate of Varce, in fact, Monsieur Mallerin had not even got round to thinking of a name for it.

Francis knew about cross-pollination, of course, but this was the very first time he had ever seen an entirely new rose; and as he stood there something stirred in him to think a man could create such fresh new loveliness – and in his own chosen calling, too. Surely to create a new rose was like creating a poem, a melody. One struggled to make reality of a dream, an ideal. And then the wonder of it! To think that in all the world there was only this one little row of that golden rose, with no name yet, no title.

And as he stooped to admire the long pointed buds, the golden yellow of the open roses, the rich green of the leaves, it was as if a sudden flame blazed within him, a flame his great-grandfather, his grand-father had known; the flame his own father, Papa Meilland, too had known, but had resolutely had to extinguish in the long hard struggle to get the business going at Tassin.

The very next morning, back again at Tassin, as soon as it was light, Francis took a new notebook and his pen, and went out into the rose-garden, and thoughtfully walked up and down between the bushes, stopping now and then to examine, consider the beauty, the scent, the qualities of this rose and that.

He finally decided on two roses: one was called 'Sunstar', a very fragrant and semi-double rose with orange and red petals and light green foliage; the other was 'Sir David Davis', another scented but double rose, a deep glowing crimson, with dark leathery green foliage. He would cross-pollinate these two, and he carefully noted down their names and added:

1 – 29.

And thus recorded that this was his first pollination of those two roses and that the year was 1929.

But 1 – 29 was also to be the first of many, many other cross-pollinations for on that red-letter day Francis Meilland, aged seventeen, became the most dedicated hybridist, always dreaming, always toiling in all his free time to create some lovely new rose – just as his great-grandfather, Joseph Rambaux, had done, and his grandfather, Francis Dubreuil, just as countless rose-lovers down the ages had done before them.

And just like all those others he too had to learn the long, hard way. There is never any smooth, short cut; it is always far from speedy and easy to create a truly worth-while new rose, one that comes up to all one's dreams and hopes.

Above all, Francis, too, had to face the hard inescapable fact that not only are the numerous offsprings of any one pair of parent roses as bewildering as the children of any one pair of human parents, all different, no two alike, but that even the most promising of the seedlings of any artificial cross-pollination are always so delicate that they require constant care and attention if they are to survive.

Not only all this but once a lovely new rose at last blooms before one's eyes it still has to be tested, proved; and then it has to be 'budded', propagated, and sold, before one earns a sou, a franc, for all the hours one has put in. And this can easily take from five to ten years!

Indeed, Papa Meilland says his heart often bled for his son in the years that followed. He was young, eager, so full of enthusiasm, but like all other hybridists before him, he too had to battle with one disheartening disappointment after another. Often, for instance, not one of the fifty or so of the most promising seedlings he had selected from the vast family of some successful cross-pollination would come up to expectation; not one would be worth budding and propagating. Another time, a whole bed of seedlings would be wiped out by mildew; another batch by some sudden and unexpected frost. And once what did his dog Caddy do but decide to bury an enormous bone right in the midst of another selection of promising but delicate young seedlings, enthusiastically scattering them high and dry to right and left as he excavated. Whereupon they promptly perished in the cold night air – all except one.

The next morning Francis, viewing this scene of ruin and destruction, shouted for Caddy, and he came bounding up barking most merrily. But drew up sharp when he saw the black look on Francis's face.

Now Caddy was not only one of those endearingly ugly and highly intelligent mongrels, and a very good if noisy watch-dog, he also knew precisely how to blackmail any human being. He only had one eye, he'd lost the other in one of his many victorious battles with lesser dogs, but he turned that solitary bright eye into a real asset. Nobody could teach Caddy a thing about 'a soft answer turneth away wrath' as he turned that one eye full of soft, bewildered love and devotion on any human poised, and braced, to give him a salutary clout.

Indeed, such was the gifted softness of Caddy's practised one eye that he was not only forgiven yet again, but when the sole survivor of that massacre got over the shock and grew into a pretty little bush of yellow roses, Francis magnanimously called it 'Caddy' and it was later propagated and sold under the name of that one-eyed dog.

This became a family joke, of course, but the hard truth was that Francis had to face one disheartening set-back and disappointment after another. Papa Meilland asked for nothing better than to help and advise Francis, but it was his mother, Claudia, who was so wonderful with their son. She was always cheerfully confident, quite sure that one day Francis would not regret all the hard work, the never-ending vexations. And she would tell him stories of the struggles of his great-grand-father, good Joseph Rambaux, and his grandfather, Francis Dubreuil, and how many times they would groan and say that one must be a lunatic to squander all one's free time cross-pollinating this rose with that one, forever lured on by some mirage. Then one day, they would forget all those long hours of work, all their blighted hopes, as they stood before some charming new rose like his great-grandfather's lovely 'Perle d'Or' for instance, or his grandfather's violet-scented 'Sarah Bernhardt'.

Then Monsieur Mallerin, too, was kindness itself. Francis would often write to him or go to Varce to discuss some new problem with him; and they would talk by the hour about the best way to rear and protect delicate, difficult young rose-seedlings. And thanks no doubt to Monsieur Mallerin – now famous in rose-growing circles for his triumphant and lovely

'Madame Pierre S. Du Pont' – little mentions of the 'promising work' of the young, unknown hybridist, Francis Meilland, began to appear in this or that magazine for rose-growers, not only in France, but in European and American journals as well.

Francis himself, of course, now always eagerly read everything on which he could lay hands about the work of famous hybridists the world over, but the one he admired most was Doctor Nicolas, who had been born in France, and had emigrated to America where he directed the Research Department of the greatest rose-growing firm in the world. Later on in life, Francis wrote:

'Each of us tries to imitate, consciously or not, the men we most admire. In my case, the "ideal" was Doctor Nicolas.'

Naturally then Francis could hardly believe his eyes when this great man also made a mention of the work 'a promising young French hybridist, Francis Meilland' was doing in Tassin, near Lyons.

Nevertheless, Francis would sometimes have a fit of black depression and sourly declare one couldn't go through life just being 'promising'. But Claudia knew how to handle her despairing son. She would briskly say, for instance, that patience wasn't precisely a virtue for a hybridist, it was a downright necessity, and that just as Rome wasn't built in a day – or so she'd read somewhere – neither was any really lovely new rose. But it was the way, the merry way, she'd bring out these time-worn clichés, making them sound so droll and yet so full of truth, that Francis would grin and say all right, all right, he'd got the message and he'd go out and see what promising prodigy he might, with luck, be propagating when he was old, wrinkled and grey.

Now this was strange but it was about this time that Rose-grower Francesco Paolino down there on the Cap d'Antibes also began to try his hand, and his luck, with cross-pollinating one rose with another.

But Rose-grower Paolino had very special and accommodating new roses in mind, ones with long, straight, strong stalks and next to no thorns, ones that would look beautiful in elegant tall cut-glass vases, and most essential of all, roses that would obligingly remain fresh, upright and lovely in their handsome vases for days on end, even in the warmest of rooms.

These new Paolino roses would make all florists sing aloud for joy, and confident as you please, they would sell them to moneyed clients, saying 'I assure you, Monsieur – or Madame – you will not regret the price! You'll be amazed how long these new roses last! Why, a lady was telling me only last week that she'd had a vase of them in her drawing-room for so long that somebody asked if they were artificial. Ha – ha – ha . . .'

So, in every free moment, Rose-grower Paolino, too, began to select and prepare and then tie little paper hats over this or that promising rose; and armed with a little brush and a supply of ripe pollen from another promising rose, he would choose the right, the precise moment to lift up some paper hat, delicately brush on a supply of pollen, and at once replace that little hat.

But these accommodating new Paolino Roses weren't in any hurry either to rush into reality. However, Rose-grower Paolino was eternally optimistic. One triumphant day there he would stand, crying 'Stupendo! Magnifico,' and shout to Marie-Elisabeth to come and behold it – the ideal, long-stemmed, long-lasting and most beautiful new Paolino rose.

As he worked he would often turn to find little Louisette standing behind him, intently watching. Then, one day she suddenly demanded a fine brush just like Papa's, a supply of pollen also like Papa's, and plenty of paper to make into little paper hats to tie over, not Papa's roses, but *her* roses' heads.

And from that day on, her Papa and Maman would often smile at each other to see their six-year-old daughter playing at being a 'lady-hybridist', and making such a picture, so pretty a picture, among all the roses.

CHAPTER NINE

Grand'mère Jenny Approves of America

In 1932, Claudia's mother peacefully died in her sleep. She was nearly eighty, so old in years, yet had she ever truly *lived* at all? How else can one explain why in the memories of all who knew her she now seems so shadowy a ghost about whom one recalls so little, so very little, apart from her infinite care of her own health, her silence, and that array of bottles of patent medicines and boxes of pills in her hushed and shuttered room.

But Claudia, always so loyal and loving, truly missed her and grieved for her, all the more so as she must have realised in her heart how much her poor Maman had always so gently and obstinately missed in life. And Papa Meilland thought it was the shock of losing her mother, her natural sorrow, that now began to make Claudia look so pale and tired. But when he suggested a visit to the doctor to ask for some good tonic, she laughed and said what nonsense; all the 'pick-me-up' she required was the rain to stop pouring down, and the wind to howl a little less dismally so that she could get out in the fresh air again and do a little tonic work among the roses.

Then came a red-letter day, a real tonic for them all. Monsieur Mallerin wrote to say he was bringing a famous American rose-grower, Mr. Robert Pyle, to Tassin. It seemed Mr. Pyle had acres of rose-gardens in Pennsylvania and that he was always on the look-out for new roses to offer his vast American clientèle.

'I've told him,' wrote Monsieur Mallerin, 'that "my student" isn't doing badly, and that he ought to meet you. But seriously, this will be an excellent opportunity for you to make your work known to a most important American rose-grower.'

Papa Meilland says the weather was still atrocious, and he well remembers the anxious preparations they made for Mr. Pyle's visit to Tassin, rigging up a little canopy to protect from the driving rain and wind the few square yards planted with the latest batch of new rose-seedlings – the only results Francis had to show for four whole years of many patient cross-pollinations and endless hours of hard work.

However, on the great day, the weather charitably changed; the sun shone out, and they whipped off the canopy from that small patch of rose-seedlings. Moreover, the famous American rose-grower was most friendly, and so easy to talk to, that Francis found himself forgetting all the dark pitfalls of English grammar and talking away most fluently in English as he brought out his stack of notebooks, the records of every one of his cross-pollinations, and the results, and all he hoped to achieve in the future with this experience now behind him. And Mr. Pyle, it seems, listened with the utmost interest.

Later on in life, Francis was to write:

'I have a feeling now that Robert Pyle was far more influenced by my youth, my enthusiasm – and the quality of my father's roses – than by what he saw in that meagre patch of unspectacular new rose-seedlings.'

But whatever it was, before he shook hands and left Tassin, Robert Pyle paid youthful Francis Meilland the best of American compliments – the offer of a contract under which he would guarantee to market in America any new rose created by Francis.

Grand'mère Jenny Approves of America

'For a beginner,' as Francis was to write later on, 'there is no greater encouragement than the proposal of a contract'; but Francis was to have a second dose of that same tonic – another offer of a contract, also from America. And this one came from Doctor Nicolas, the famous hybridist, the man Francis had always so warmly admired, his 'ideal'.

Francis walked on air. Two offers of contracts from two such important men in the rose-growing world! And both hard-headed business men; one had to be *that*, over there in America. So this was a real gesture of faith in him, Francis Meilland, who as yet, in spite of all his hard work, had not a single new rose to his credit.

Papa Meilland and Claudia, of course, rejoiced with their son. In fact, Papa Meilland brought out one of his best bottles, reserved for special occasions, and they drank to the health of those two discerning, distinguished American rose-lovers, and all other rose-lovers, too, wherever they were.

It was tragic, heart-breaking, but it was now, so soon after the death of her aged, ailing mother, when the rose-gardens they had struggled so hard to establish were at last going well, with regular orders coming in from all over France and other European countries, too, when Francis was beginning to be recognised as a most outstanding young hybridist, that Claudia had to fight so hard not to show how tired and unwell she was feeling. And what pain she often had to endure.

Her age, she told herself. Everyone knew that women had to put up with all manner of discomforts at a certain time of life. One simply had to endure all this and in time Nature put everything right. She, too, would be her old self one of these days. And maybe because of the haunting memory of her eternally ailing mother, Claudia fought tooth and nail never to betray how ill, how tired she felt, and how racked at times with pain.

God only knows how valiantly she fought, and what a bitter blow it was to Papa Meilland to find her one day, lying on a little path between the rose-beds, grey with pain and sudden exhaustion.

As he carried her to her bed, she tried to laugh at his concern, saying, of course, she hadn't fallen down, she had only been having a little rest, and that she would be perfectly all right in a day or so.

But Claudia was never again to laugh and sing as she worked in the gardens among the roses she loved so dearly. It had not been her age. She was ill, incurably ill, and there was nothing that their doctor, or the finest specialist in all Lyons could do for her – except mercifully alleviate her pain.

And as she lay dying, it broke Papa Meilland's heart to hear her rambling in her delirium of saving up now and going down there to the Côte d'Azur, to the Cap d'Antibes for a holiday; and sitting in the sunshine, seeing the mimosas in bloom, the palm trees, the orange and lemon trees, and the warm blue sea.

Then Papa Meilland would take her hand and swear they would go, of course they would go.

Never once since that long-ago evening had Claudia ever mentioned that holiday, maybe because they always had to be so frugal and thrifty, maybe because her kind heart would not let her think of leaving her ailing mother for more than a day.

And the bitter irony of it all was now her mother was dead, now things were at last going well, they could indeed have started to save for that longed-for holiday. But there lay Claudia, dying, talking of nothing but the sunshine, the mimosas in golden bloom, and the warm blue sea she would never now see.

Grand'mère Jenny Approves of America

In all those agonising days, Grand'mère Jenny was a tower of strength. And just before she died, Claudia opened her eyes and in a God-given moment of clarity, recognised her. It was almost as if she knew she would be there, by her bed; and she seemed to gather up all her strength to speak.

'Grand'mère Jenny, je vous laisse mes deux hommes . . .'

'Grand'mère Jenny, I leave you my two men . . .'

Grand'mère Jenny took her thin hand in her courageous old hand and held it tight, but could find no words.

Claudia understood, for she smiled; and then was lost again in delirium. And that night, less than a year after the death of her mother, Claudia died. She was only forty.

Then the whole world about Papa Meilland and Francis froze, most desolate and empty. And heaven only knows what would have happened to them both if Grand'mère Jenny had not been there, setting meals before them and peremptorily ordering them to eat. She did even more; she began to take Francis to one side and sternly say he must think of his poor Papa and insist that he went away with him for a few days' rest.

Then when Francis was out of the way, she would tackle Papa Meilland and say, believe her, she knew how he must be feeling, none better, but he must think of his son and take the poor lad away for a few days' rest.

This, coming from Grand'mère Jenny, staggered them both. Never before on any occasion had she ever seen the necessity for anyone to take a holiday. Never once, until then.

And one couldn't argue with Grand'mère Jenny, above all then. And giving them no chance, no time to hesitate, she packed off her son and grandson as if they had been children to take that few days' rest – in sunny Antibes.

Grand'mère Jenny did not add – Claudia would have wished it. There was no need. They knew it was true, that this is just what Claudia herself would have wished. And there was no shaking off this feeling. So Papa Meilland and Francis picked up the valise and the sandwiches that Grand'mère Jenny had ready for them to eat on the train, and went. Down there to Antibes.

When Papa Meilland opened his eyes that first morning in Antibes and looked bleakly around the neat little hotel bedroom, he swears it was his guardian angel who must have suggested that they ought to call on Monsieur Francesco Paolino, their old and valued client. It would only be polite, and it would make them *do* something, make them find their voices again, shake them out of their desolate, tired thoughts.

And one must certainly give full marks to Papa Meilland's guardian angel for it seems that little Madame Paolino took one look at their black suits, their haggard unhappy faces, and promptly sent her dark-eyed pretty little daughter Louisette racing into the garden to fetch her Papa. And within a quarter of an hour, they were sitting, refreshments before them, on a shady terrace, smiling for the first time in many weeks.

Then, taking no notice whatever of their protestations that they had only come to pay their compliments, to have the pleasure of meeting Monsieur and Madame Paolino at last, little Madame Paolino was bustling round crying, what, stay in an hotel! The very idea! Hadn't they known one another by post, and catalogues, all these years, and forgive her, but this wasn't Lyons, one didn't stand on ceremony down here, at least the Paolinos didn't. They were always enchanted to have visitors, such a splendid reason to sit around and talk. So not another word, she would send someone for their valise, their beds were already made up for them, and they must tell her what they thought of the 'pasta asciutta' she would make them presently. They could never have tasted anything like this up there in Lyons. One had to be taught by her Mamma-in-law Paolino to achieve this Italian master-piece. And laughing away, she told the story of that detestable dog, Perla.

All of which goes to show, of course, that little Madame Paolino had not changed. She was still the same generous, spontaneous little Marie-Elisabeth who gave away that one daily sou, always forgetting her Maman's plaintive cry, 'But one is not rich, I tell you! One is not rich.'

And thank God she had not changed, for this was precisely what they most needed, this gay warm hospitality, this lack of all ceremony, this being swept into another world, and above all this being made to feel they were so very welcome.

Those few days' rest in Antibes could have been so un-bearable, above all for Papa Meilland now seeing for the first time the blue sea, the orange and lemon trees, the mimosas, all that Claudia had so longed to see. He would have given his very soul to have had her there at his side.

But they were given no time, no chance to sit forlornly, lost in regret and sorrow. And the wonder of it, thought Papa Meilland, that he and Francesco Paolino, two men outwardly so unalike, with such different backgrounds, should get on together so famously after their very first handshake – he, Antoine Meilland, over six feet tall in his socks, a solid sober son of Chamboeuf if ever there was one, and volatile 'piccolo' Francesco Paolino, talking away to him in fluent French, very Provençal French, with a warm strong Italian tang to it. It warmed one's heart just to listen to him.

The bridge between them, of course, was their love of roses, and soon Papa Meilland and Francis were inspecting the Paolino rose-garden, and hearing how it had been literally hewn from the wild tangled forest. And Papa Meilland had to hand it to him, Rose-grower Francesco Paolino might be 'piccolo' – pint-sized – but no one had more impeccable, more beautifully tended gardens. But then, as Papa Meilland says, he already knew what artists, what workers, these Italians were, having seen those merry chair-makers at work in Chamboeuf when he was a child.

Moreover, Rose-grower Paolino was not content with gardens alone. He now had greenhouses as well, if you please, so that he had roses in bloom, and for sale, the whole year round. Yes, those Paolino gardens and greenhouses were an eye-opener, a real pleasure to inspect; and Papa Meilland is not given to easy compliments, least of all about roses.

Then little Madame Paolino could not only cook like her Mamma-in-law Paolino, but she obviously revelled in having visitors; and they would sit out on the terrace after supper of an evening, drinking her excellent coffee, and Papa Meilland would hear himself laugh, a sound he thought he would never again hear, as they listened to tales of Papa the Corporal, and Mamma Paolino and her mass-produced dresses, and her masterly handling of her turbulent family and High Finance, all of which had paid such handsome dividends in the end.

It seemed Papa the Corporal and Mamma Paolino had finished their time on this earth in a veritable blaze of parental pride and triumph, knowing that every Paolino by birth or marriage was working hard and doing well – and the two don't always walk hand in hand. It was Mamma who had died first; her last thoughts were all for her many grandchildren, but Papa the Corporal, the head of the family, had lived on until he was well over ninety, doing his soldierly best to represent the good God in the family to the very end.

Ah yes, the world would be a better saner place, said little Marie-Elisabeth, if all parents were cut of the same cloth as Papa the Corporal and Mamma Paolino.

Grand'mère Jenny Approves of America

Then it was absorbing too, to compare notes and discover how two boys, one up there in Chamboeuf, and one down here in Antibes, had so doggedly determined to spend their lives growing roses. And how Francesco Paolino, now sitting there to tell the tale, had first become a 'Cordonnier, Maître Bottier', a specialist, though he said so himself, in making elegant shoes with a built-in 'cric-crac-cric-crac'; and magnificently giving credit to one and all, till CRACK, he was declared a bankrupt – his first decisive step to becoming a rose-grower though he didn't precisely recommend this method to any future generation of rose-growers.

But Papa Meilland had also, it seemed, been far the more fortunate lad, for he'd served his time as apprentice to an expert arborist, whereas young Rose-grower Paolino had to learn where and how he could. And he didn't mind confessing it now, but at first he had naïvely relied for professional advice on a certain character who swaggered away about his profound knowledge of the right, and most profitable way to prune all trees, especially roses. And he had respectfully treated this character to more than one drink, reverently listening to all his instructions.

But that character was either the world's finest liar or a black-hearted scoundrel who thought it a prime joke to delude a young fool trying to grow roses out there in the wild woods of the Cap, for his pruning instructions had proved disastrous, almost the death of Francesco's first cherished beds of young rose-bushes.

But Francesco Paolino had again learned a lesson. After that, he trusted only his own two good eyes, minutely watching skilled gardeners at work as they pruned the roses in the Municipal Gardens of Antibes and Nice.

This talk of gardens, of course, led to Marie-Elisabeth telling them of the wonderful estate of Madame la Baronne Alice de

Rothschild in Grasse where one could tell the rank and importance of any man in her vast hierarchy of gardeners by the colour of the beret he wore on his head.

And so, to and fro, and back down the years, went the memories, the friendly talk until they felt they had known one another all their lives long; and when those few days were over, Papa Meilland and Francis, looking much better, went back to Tassin, faithfully promising to remember they would always be welcome down there on the Cap.

And Rose-grower Paolino faithfully promised to travel up there to Tassin one day; he fully intended to prowl round those Meilland gardens, use his eyes, and pick up a few tips from Papa Meilland and this up-and-coming hybridist son of his.

Francis, sitting in the train, heading back to Lyons, thought about little Louisette Paolino, how gravely she had considered him in silence before she decided to begin to talk to him. And how quick and intelligent she had turned out to be, asking such apt questions about the work he was doing, and listening so intently when he explained.

And she made such a charming picture in her gay little dress out there in the sunshine among her Papa's roses. She also had the most fascinating accent, real Provençal; it was amusing just to listen to her.

Then he thought how one day they had stood looking across the rose-beds at the sun setting over the sea, and the beauty of it had loosened his tongue and he had suddenly blurted out how his mother had so longed to see all this.

She was silent for a moment. She didn't even turn her head. And then she quietly said, 'This must be like a pilgrimage for you and your father.'

Francis was dumbfounded. It was true, of course, but how

strange that a child of twelve should be so swiftly, so instinctively perceptive.

Yes. Louisette was most unusual. And very pretty. He liked her.

Louisette, however, was thinking how stiff and formal this young man from Lyons had been at first, gravely looking at her in silence, weighing her up, before he decided to risk conversing with a twelve-year-old girl who might be given to fits of alarming giggles. He hadn't any sisters of his own, of course. One could tell that. And he was quite elderly, over twenty, in fact, eight years older than she was.

But he was quite pleasant, decided Louisette, once he thawed, and one got to know him a little better. And that Lyonnais accent of his was fascinating, it was amusing just to listen to him.

He was also well-informed, a real help on the night Louisette had struggled with her English home-work, those impossible English irregular verbs: 'to behold', 'to begin', and 'to sell'.

And he had laughed and said only the English could explain, if they ever explained anything at all, why it is so correct to say, 'I walk, I walked. I finish, I finished,' but never, never, 'I behold, I beholded. I begin, I beginned. I sell, I selled.' That was *most* incorrect. One had to say, 'I behold, I beheld. I begin, I began,' and craziest of all, 'I sell, I sold.'

Yes, doing her English home-work that evening had been positively entertaining.

And Louisette decided she quite liked Francis Meilland, and not only because of his useful knowledge of English verbs. He was also very nice – in an elderly way, of course.

The morning after their return to Tassin, Papa Meilland and Francis plunged headlong into the work waiting for them in the rose-garden; and Grand'mère Jenny, washing up the breakfast things, and planning what to cook for their meals that day, paused for a moment to thank heaven they both looked so much better for those few days away. She also thanked wise heaven they had so much work on hand waiting to be done. Nothing so healing as good hard work as she had proved for herself when her own poor man had died and left her alone on their farm.

Grand'mère Jenny abruptly wiped her eyes and blew her nose, and if she was also grieving for that little farm at Chamboeuf, sold now, she refused to admit it, not even to herself. She was keeping her unspoken promise to Claudia.

'I leave you my two men . . .'

And that was what Grand'mère Jenny intended to do, look after those two men.

She also decided she had better start a 'basse-cour' – keep some fowls and a good masterful cock to keep them in order. She'd have a few rabbits too; and take over the vegetable garden. Grand'mère Jenny's favourite saying was: 'One should *see* what one gives one's family to eat, see it growing.'

In her free time she would also lend a hand in the rose-garden, of course.

Oh, she'd be kept busy enough. She wouldn't have a moment to be homesick for Chamboeuf.

Home was here now at Tassin, with those two helpless men.

In 1935, Francis Meilland made a decision that staggered everyone they knew, indeed it was considered by some to be completely out of place, positively vainglorious for an ordinary working rose-grower, even if he were a promising young hybridist as well.

As for Grand'mère Jenny, she acidly said the lad must be crazy, and one would at least expect his father to show some sense, stamp with both his big feet on so hare-brained an idea, not sit there calmly listening.

To Grand'mère Jenny's horror, Francis had counted up all his savings, the proceeds of the sale of chickweed, holly, mistletoe, ruscus and all those far more profitable young peach-trees, and had decided to squander the lot on a trip to America. America!

Papa Meilland says one must understand that Grand'mère Jenny was only feeling as any loving granny would feel to-day to hear her young grandson declare he was about to blue all his savings, with his foolhardy father's permission, on a return trip by rocket to the moon.

In those days young people did not set off, as happy-go-lucky as you please, to travel to the other side of the world on a shoe-string. Even a trip to Paris was a sensation, the experience of a life-time. Francis had never once been even that far from home. Yet there he was, determined to go to America and see how one grew roses there.

And that, Grand'mère Jenny darkly and most unjustly commented, was what came of a lad eternally sticking his nose of an evening in all those American journals with photographs of skyscrapers as tall as the Tower of Babel and every Christian knew what had happened to *that*.

And Grand'mère Jenny had soon sharply silenced everyone's clacking tongue, of course, but all the same it didn't make for her peace of mind to learn that there were some who were not only shaking their heads, too, over this wild extravagance, they were actually declaring:

'Il va mettre son père sur la paille.'

'He'll have his father sleeping on straw.'

Oh yes, said Grand'mère Jenny, some were already darkly prophesying that if Francis went on like this, he'd ruin his father, reduce him to dire poverty.

But Papa Meilland was remembering how Claudia always said, 'You'll see! It will all come in useful one day!' every time Francis added a little to his savings.

He remembered how dearly she, too, would have loved to travel; and when the chance at last came, it had come too late.

Above all, he remembered that evening when Francis, setting out to learn English Language and Literature in Lyons, had turned in the doorway and declared he now had a feeling he would one day travel round the world. And Claudia had so gravely smiled as if to say:

'But of course! Why not?'

So Papa Meilland turned a deaf ear to all the local Cassandras, and said, 'Why not?' just as Claudia would have wished. But he naturally gave his son a few sober words of fatherly advice and warning, and one April morning Francis set out for America, his face shining like the sun, his savings stowed away in an innermost pocket, and solemnly assuring Grand'mère Jenny that he would devour three good American meals a day, keep his eyes skinned for American pickpockets and gangsters, and make straight for the White House in Washington and demand redress, in the name of Lafayette, from the President of the United States himself if he was ever robbed of those savings or ran into any other American disaster.

Papa Meilland says one required a map of the whole continent of North America to keep up with his globe-trotting son. He was away two months and he covered 15,000 miles; and he never once forgot to write home long, long letters setting down all he had done and seen.

Papa Meilland regrets to say his son didn't think much of the Statue of Liberty. Her green stern face looked positively menacing to him as if she, too, dared him to get robbed of his savings.

But New York fascinated him though his money wouldn't permit more than an economical gallop round all the usual towering sights, especially as he had decided, if you please, that it would be far cheaper, and more attractive, to 'do' America in a car, and not by train. And that 'Innocent Abroad', as Mark Twain would have certainly put it, bought himself a second-hand American car, and, with his young heart thumping like a drum, he drove it down an incline from the eighth floor – that New York garage was also a skyscraper, of course – and plunged straight into the traffic roaring along Broadway, yes, Broadway, his hair standing on end and praying he hadn't been swindled and that he was heading in the right direction.

His prayer was answered. He had not been swindled. On the contrary that second-hand car chugged along like some sturdy good-natured sewing-machine; and soon he was eating up the miles all round the United States and down to Mexico, calling on all the best-known professional rose-growers as he went.

Some of them, Mr. Robert Pyle, for instance, and Doctor Nicolas, already knew who he was; others remembered reading an odd paragraph about him in some trade journal; but even if they had never heard of him, they all received him with the most generous and friendly American kindness.

They took time off to show him what they were doing, they explained their methods of working, and Papa Meilland says those American rose-growers were like their skyscrapers – they took one's breath away by the gigantic scale of their rose-growing. They grew vast prairies, not gardens, of roses and they had invented the most incredible of labour-saving machines. And this tickled Papa Meilland, Francis wrote that one of these vast American firms had found it so difficult and expensive to obtain good manure for their acres of roses that they invested in a fine placid herd of cows, two hundred and fifty of them, to meet their rose-growing requirements.

There they grazed, wrote Francis, those contented cows, on a vast green prairie of their own, and all about them bloomed those scented acres of well-fertilised roses. What more could an American cow or rose ask of life?

Then back to New York drove Francis, and almost wept to part from that second-hand American car – it had been so loyal and trustworthy a friend, never once letting him down. And that American garage, too, was one hundred per cent reliable. They took the car back at the agreed price, which was just as well, for though Francis had received the utmost generous hospitality, his savings had all but vanished. Even that splendid car couldn't run on air, and he had covered those 15,000 miles.

Fortunately, too, he had prudently booked and paid in advance for his return trip to France.

So back, safe and sound, to Tassin came the traveller, his head spinning with all he had seen and his valise crammed with American rose-catalogues with superb coloured illustrations that made them real works of art, a delight to study, even if one hadn't a garden in which to plant the roses they pictured. And he'd also filled notebook upon notebook with details about labour-saving machines that made spades look like pre-historic tools; not to mention American cold stores where one maintained by automatic control the temperature and humidity so efficiently that one could store all one's rose-bushes, roots exposed, the whole winter long with no risk, no fear whatever that they might dry out, or die of cold.

All of which 'Meilland and Son', too, would invest in – when they had the necessary cash, of course.

But this impressed Francis most of all. In America a hybridist who brought out any new variety of plant or flower could apply for a patent and so become legally entitled to a fair percentage of all the sales, the profits, made on his new creation – for seventeen years! In America, a hybridist certainly reaped the just rewards of his labour.

Now this did not appeal to Francis only because he himself was a dedicated hybridist, it appealed above all to his sense of justice. If hybridists were legally protected from 'piracy' in America, why not everywhere else?

But Papa Meilland pointed out that one would have to engage and pay multi-lingual lawyers to argue the case maybe for years in every country outside America, and what poor devil of a European hybridist, who also had a living to earn and a family to support, could ever afford to do that?

No, it might be plain justice, said Papa Meilland, that every hybridist should reap a fair share of the rewards of his labours, but outside America it was a lofty, unobtainable, a far too costly ideal.

And it seemed Francis looked at him and said one had talked precisely like that in the past about so many other wrongs that had now been put right.

The morning after his return to Tassin, Grand'mère Jenny, shaking a duster from a bedroom window, smiled for the first time in two whole months. Out there, bright and early, their wanderer in his blue gardener's outfit was already at work among the roses. And Grand'mère Jenny told herself she had been a silly old woman to worry so, and never again would she believe all those horror-stories about gangsters in America. Why, a lad and his savings were as safe and welcome there as in Tassin or Chamboeuf. And one had to admit, he could also see and learn a great deal more.

And from that day on, Grand'mère Jenny's heart was very warm and apologetic to far-away America. She had, of course, kept all the picture postcards Francis had sent her, but the one she liked best was the Statue of Liberty. Grand'mère Jenny thoroughly approved of the stern look on the face of that upright and modestly clad woman. In fact, she considered they could well do with a statue like that up there in Paris instead of that ridiculous and costly Tour Eiffel.

CHAPTER TEN

'Golden State'

The following year, 1936, Francis, fired by his visit to America, persuaded Papa Meilland to risk the extra expense of including a few gay pages of coloured illustrations in their modest sober black and white catalogue. They were the very first rose-growers in Europe to do this, and the immediate result was most gratifying – or so it seemed at first.

To their surprise they were promptly approached by a very large wholesale firm which annually sold many thousands of rose-bushes; and they made them a splendid offer – an excellent contract. But this contract called, however, for a complete revision of their usual programme.

Up to then, their catalogue had always offered a choice of three hundred varieties of roses, but under this contract they would have to concentrate on only thirty best selling varieties and also increase their total output by one-third. Then this wholesale firm would buy the lot, or as Francis enthusiastically put it, for once they would sell right out, not have a single rose-bush left on their hands unsold. And in the end he persuaded his conservative Papa to accept this splendid offer and sign this attractive contract.

So they concentrated on those thirty varieties only, and slaved to bud one-third more bushes than they had ever done before. And that meant working overtime at the gallop, Papa

Meilland can tell you. However, they completed the programme
dead on time, and as they triumphantly surveyed that gigantic
crop of thirty varieties of roses, the firm which had made
this splendid contract with them went bankrupt! Most devasta-
tingly bankrupt!

And there they were with all that army of thirty varieties
of rose-bushes left on their hands.

No other wholesale firm anywhere in France would be
capable, even if they were willing, to buy and dispose of such
a multitude. So, as Papa Meilland mournfully said, it was a
case of either burning the lot or trying to sell them themselves.
And very sales-inspiring that would look to be sure! They
now only had thirty varieties of roses, not three hundred, to
offer their clients. A splendid catalogue that would make,
and no mistake. No customers would be satisfied with so
meagre a choice.

No, said Papa Meilland gloomily, the outlook was black
to the point of bankruptcy. And this is what came of accepting,
without smelling a rat, a far too glittering offer.

However, Francis, still fired by America, refused to be
pessimistic. On the contrary, he maintained the situation was
unique, an exceptional opportunity. They alone would have a
sensational stock of excellent bushes of thirty varieties of the
best-selling roses. And he now enthusiastically persuaded his
pessimistic, conservative Papa into a second gamble – a
publicity campaign as in America, an unheard of strategy for
rose-growers in France in those days. And Papa Meilland not
only had a horror of all gambles but this second one was to
the tune of 37,000 francs, a vast sum of money then. For this
alarming outlay they were to have a supply of magnificent
coloured posters, and what seemed to Papa Meilland ton upon
ton of costly catalogues illustrating in lovely colour every one
of those thirty varieties of roses.

Captivated, enchanted by all this novel and colourful publicity, Francis positively saw the orders pouring in for their great crop of roses.

The trouble was, however, that for all his two months in America, Francis had no experience whatever of organising a high-powered, fast-moving publicity campaign; and Papa Meilland, of course, knew even less. And their first, all-important shot at one started off at a veritable crawl. In fact, there was one time-wasting delay after another. The printers, for instance, seemed to need dynamite to get them and their presses going; and Francis could no longer disguise his anxiety and apprehension when, in that autumn of 1937, all their competitors had not only sent out their good safe black and white catalogues, they had also dispatched every one of their orders, completed all their sales, and 'Meilland and Son' hadn't even seen, much less sent out a single catalogue, not one expensive poster.

Time grew shorter and shorter; and as Papa Meilland irately pointed out, everyone would soon have bought all the rose-bushes they were likely to require. The possibility of disposing of their record crop grew more and more unlikely, and still those costly coloured catalogues, those high-priced posters had not turned up from the printers. Thoroughly alarmed now, Papa Meilland sternly warned Francis that he would give him another fortnight and then, if all those tons of paper hadn't been delivered, and dispatched, he would forthwith, and for ever, lose all confidence both in his son *and* in his brilliant new American business-methods. In fact, thundered Papa Meilland, they'd be lucky if they themselves didn't go bankrupt and find themselves 'sleeping on the straw'.

But, thank heaven, just before that fateful fortnight was up, their local Post Office was snowed under with an avalanche of multicoloured catalogues and posters. And out and away all over France and Europe they went by post and Papa Meilland and Francis sat uneasily back, held their breath, and offered up a silent prayer.

The result was magnificent, wonderful. Twenty-three days later they hadn't one rose-bush left for sale. In fact, they had to rush out a circular of apology to a multitude of would-be customers. The disaster had been transformed to spectacular success.

Papa Meilland says he was staggered. He had thought it so unlikely that there could be anyone at all left at that late moment who would still want to order and buy a new rose-bush. But this publicity campaign had proved he was wrong, utterly mistaken. It had reached out and discovered a whole, most unexpected market of clients who had been enchanted to study a beautiful coloured catalogue, specialising in and listing only thirty carefully selected varieties of roses.

Francis thoughtfully said this was highly significant. But all Papa Meilland gratefully thought was that they had been spared the misery of burning all those excellent bushes, that they could now pay that nightmare of a bill from the printers. And that far from being reduced to 'sleeping on the straw', they could face their Bank Manager with a sunny, confident smile all over their faces, and go to sleep of a night in their good comfortable beds.

But this also strangely moved Papa Meilland: it was not the first time that a rose-catalogue had played so unexpected, so rewarding a part in his life. No, this was not the first time.

Now all the while, come rain come shine, in every moment of his free time Francis had been carrying on with his search for a new and lovely rose. Eight years had gone by since that first cross-pollination, 1 – 29, eight long years of sowing many thousands of tiny seeds, eight years of careful observation and selecting, and most difficult of all, caring for one batch after another of promising but delicate and capricious young rose-seedlings.

So you may imagine how Francis felt as year after year went by and in spite of all his patient, hard work, he still had no new rose to his credit. This doesn't mean, however, that never once from all these cross-pollinations had he seen any lovely new rose come into bloom. He most certainly had. But no matter how beautiful a new rose was, he knew better than to rush it straight out on the market on the strength of one first glorious blooming. He then had to test it, prove its lasting value, by letting it grow and bloom for two or three years, sometimes longer, in a trial-bed' in their garden.

And year after year Francis had to face the same bitter disappointment – even the most promising and charming of his new roses would later betray signs of some disastrous weakness, some serious shortcoming. In fact, one day Francis morosely told Papa Meilland that not one of the new roses he slaved to create ever behaved like a certain 'wise thrush', a real virtuoso, who it seemed had never failed to send the English poet, Robert Browning, into transports of delight – in beautiful verse, of course. Unlike that 'wise thrush', his new roses 'never could recapture that first fine careless rapture'. On the contrary, after sending his hopes soaring high with their 'first fine careless' blooming, there was only one word to sum up their subsequent performance – heartbreaking.

However, he worked doggedly on, and at last, in 1937, eight years after that first cross-pollination, Francis triumphantly presented his first new rose, a glorious yellow one, deep cupped, double, and with magnificent, glossy foliage. It had been carefully tested and tried not only in their own 'trial beds' but in the 'trial beds' of other interested professional rose-growers in France and other European countries; and a supply had also been sent out to be tested by Mr. Robert Pyle, who had so optimistically had faith in an unknown and eager young French hybridist, and had given him so warm a welcome on that memorable trip to America. And every one of these experts was now definitely enchanted by this first new rose.

But as yet it had no name, for again they had to be cautious. They had faithful and friendly clients in other lands and they knew that a name may strike just the right note in one language but mean nothing at all in another. Worse still, it may be positively off-putting, or even comical.

Say 'Pigalle', for instance, to anyone who knows and loves Paris and ten to one they won't give a thought to Jean-Baptiste Pigalle, the eighteenth-century sculptor responsible for some of the grandiose monuments one sees here and there in Paris. No, to them, the name 'Pigalle' immediately conjures up that gay Parisian square: 'La Place Pigalle', where nobody ever seems inclined to go to bed of a night.

So to them, 'Pigalle' might seem a gay rollicking name for a gay rollicking new rose, but to many others the first three letters are definitely off-putting. 'Pig'! Ah, no!

Then someone else, remembering 'Anitra's Dance' in Peer Gynt, once thought 'Anitra' would be just the name for a new rose, till Italian rose-growers guffawed and said, ah no, it was far too close to 'Anatra', the Italian for duck.

And as Papa Meilland puts it, delicious and first-class as 'Lord Pig' or a prime roast duck may be, one nevertheless hardly associates them with some lovely, graceful rose. Indeed, when it comes to choosing a name for a new rose, the old French adage is literally true:

'A good name is better than a gold belt.' In fact, Papa Meilland himself would amend that to:

'A good name, for a rose, is better than any gold medal.'

After much discussion, it was decided to leave the name of

the new rose to Mr. Robert Pyle. And Papa Meilland says he sure took their breath away. He launched that new golden-yellow French rose on the American market with all the publicity trumpets sounding, under the name of 'Golden State' – a name they would never have dreamed of themselves, and it was then triumphantly adopted as the official emblem of the great San Francisco International Exhibition.

In a nutshell, it was a rip-roaring success. 'As a trial, a first new rose, it is a masterpiece,' wrote one admiring American journalist. He didn't add, by the way, that this 'trial' had taken eight long years to achieve. But what matter? Francis, too, completely forgot this when his first new rose went on to win first place in three of the greatest international contests, and dearer, better far, to Papa Meilland's patriotic heart, that same year it won the much envied title:

La plus belle rose de France.

The most beautiful rose of France.

Then still at whirlwind speed, in to Tassin began to roll the most welcome of American dollars. Mr. Pyle had, of course, promptly taken out a patent for 'Golden State', and this meant that on every bush sold anywhere in the United States, Francis received a certain percentage.

And did Francis prudently save those American dollars? He did not. To everyone's amazement he invested the lot in realising the first of his dreams – the building of a cold store just like the ones he had admired so in America, and in which all their rose-bushes could now safely pass even the most bitter of winters. It was the first to be built this side of the Atlantic, and it just about soaked up all that welcome avalanche of dollars. But presently, there it stood – a solid gesture of faith in the future. And you may be sure that there were many more shakings of the head and dark mutterings that if young Francis Meilland went on like this, 'il va mettre son père sur la paille!' that was certain. All those American dollars sunk for ever in a cold store, and for rose-bushes of all things!

Grand'mère Jenny, busy from morning till night, also had her dark doubts about spending all those American dollars in this wholesale way. What would her poor man have thought of it? As if she didn't know . . . His hair would have stood straight on end on his head. 'One can't *eat* roses,' he would have said, haunted eternally by the cruel, gnawing hunger of that long-ago Franco-Prussian War.

And very sharp-tongued and impatient she had been at times with her poor man. And here she was now, airing her doubts, all unasked, on the folly of spending so much money on a store . . . for roses.

Then Grand'mère Jenny, not for the first time, told heaven it was high time her grandson took time off from his roses and cold store, and looked around for a suitable wife. But she warned heaven it would have its celestial job cut out to find the right girl for *this* house. She would have to be devoted to roses as well as to her husband. Otherwise, as Grand'mère Jenny warned heaven, there could be no lasting happiness for either of them, no real harmony. In *this* house, a young wife might well become jealous of roses – of all things!

Then Grand'mère Jenny told heaven that she knew, none better, that she was a sharp-tongued old woman, forever rapping out orders, even to heaven, but someone had to see those two men sat down to good meals, had clean shirts, and had their socks darned; and she would so dearly like a kind, rose-loving wife for Francis, someone who would make a good affectionate daughter-in-law to his Papa, someone to whom, when the time came, Grand'mère Jenny would in her turn peacefully leave those two men. Amen. Amen.

But nobody, not Grand'mère Jenny, Papa Meilland and

certainly not Francis himself, had any idea of what heaven still had in store for them in that golden year, 1937.

Francis was looking pale and tired; he always worked very long hours and now there had been the heavy extra responsibility of supervising the building of their costly cold store, so Papa Meilland and Grand'mère Jenny between them persuaded him to take a few days off, have a short rest – down there on the Cap d'Antibes.

Since that first friendly meeting five years ago with the family Paolino they had always kept in touch, and Francis had sent them letters and picture postcards from America, of course, and every time they replied, there would always be a postscript:

'But when are you going to find the time to come down and see us again? The door is wide open.'

Louisette was fifteen when Francis made that memorable trip to America and she had kept all his letters and cards, saying one never knew, they might come in useful for a girl's geography homework one of these days. She had even brought out and studied her atlas – a thing she had never voluntarily done before – to follow Francis Meilland chugging away in his second-hand car, lapping up 15,000 miles of America and Mexico.

She also secretly thought Francis Meilland had a wonderful way of describing everything. In fact, she decided Fabre, the great French naturalist, couldn't have done better than Francis Meilland when he wrote how he sank down on a bench one day in a beautiful and enormous park in the city of Washington, worn out with gazing at majestic monuments white as the driven snow. And instantly down from the trees all about him flew blue thrushes, yes, blue ones, and flocks of impudent sparrows and outsize swaggering robins, twice as big and bold and red as any European ones.

At first they politely hopped around as if to say:

'That's right, Mister. You sit down and take it easy. Now turn out your pockets. You've surely brought us hungry birds a peck of something or the other.'

And they crowded about his feet, jostling and chattering, this one giving his trousers an encouraging flick of a wing, that one an impatient peck, and louder and louder grew the din as if they were shouting one another down and calling to him:

'Aw, come on, Mister! A bird hasn't got all day. Bread will do if you haven't any cookies.'

Then across the green grass danced a grey squirrel, bull-dozed his way through the outraged chattering birds, jumped on the bench, and straight on Francis's knee.

That did it. Up on the bench now flew the sparrows, the blue thrushes and robins, angrily protesting at this gangster gate-buster, till suddenly, from heaven knows where, another grey squirrel appeared, sized up the situation in a flash, and up he sprang, too, on Francis's other knee.

Straightaway the sparrows, the blue thrushes and the robins made a mass attack. If anybody was going to sit on this guy's knees, they were going to have that pleasure, they, his 'feathered friends'. They'd been the first to spot him.

Suddenly, as if menaced by some terrible disaster, the two squirrels took off, undoubtedly squeaking: 'Beat it! Beat it! Danger! Danger!'

They put on such a performance that even the outsize swaggering robins took fright, and up and away flew all Francis's 'feathered friends'.

Then back danced the two squirrels, sprang straight on Francis's knees, and waited for the applause. And the few biscuits he most fortunately had in his pocket.

Louisette had quite enjoyed, too, reading about the day Francis took off from American rose-growing to visit the Falls of Niagara. He had also sent her a couple of picture postcards of this magnificent sight, writing on the backs such interesting information as:

'500,000 cubic metres of water fall every minute from a height of fifty metres.'

As if a girl wanted to know unpoetical facts like that! She was also amused and indignant – as one often is with the factual elderly – when he wrote that it was most impressive when this gigantic waterfall was illuminated at night with a blaze of dazzling white light from powerful projectors on the Canadian side of the Falls. But that he had at first winced, then had to laugh his head off, when the Falls suddenly became a lurid 'washer-woman blue' and then an impossible 'crème-de-menthe'.

But fifteen-year-old Louisette thought those Falls must have looked altogether out of this world, absolutely spell-binding, changing colour like this, 500,000 cubic metres of magical water falling down fifty enchanted metres. That's how she herself would have seen this Transformation Spectacle. But then, of course, one wouldn't expect someone of Francis's age to appreciate the wonder of it.

Two years had gone by since those cards and letters had arrived in Antibes from America, and Louisette wasn't so sure now about the magical beauty of seeing the Niagara Falls turn 'washer-woman blue' and 'crème-de-menthe'. But she certainly was pleased Francis Meilland was coming to see them again; she'd like to hear more about America and romantic Mexico.

It seems Francis was stunned, completely taken-aback when he again set eyes on Louisette. He had expected, as one always does, to see her maybe a shade taller, but still a child. She was nothing of the sort. She was a charming and lovely girl of seventeen. She had grown up. She was beautiful, truly beautiful.

Louisette, too, was secretly taken-aback. Why, Francis Meilland wasn't elderly at all. He was a most likeable and presentable young man not yet twenty-five. Yes, quite young, and quite good-looking. And very witty and entertaining.

You can guess the rest. Francis Meilland fell head over heels in love with Louisette Paolino; and she with him.

And all around them bloomed roses, thousands of roses, which, of course, was just as it should be for any pair of young lovers, above all for the daughter of Francesco Paolino, and the son of Antoine Meilland.

CHAPTER ELEVEN

3 — 35 — 40

On January 14th, 1939, Louisette Paolino married Francis
Meilland in the Chapelle Saint Benoit on the Cap d'Antibes.

Her Maman naturally thought Louisette made the most
beautiful of brides in her lovely white satin dress, her long
bridal veil, and carrying an enchanting bouquet – white roses,
of course, all hand-picked by her Papa. And glancing around
at the well-dressed, smiling guests, the bride's little Maman
wished Papa the Corporal and Mamma Paolino could have
lived to see this wedding. It would have made them positively
shine with pride to see their sons and daughters with their
wives, husbands, children and some of them now with grandchildren of their own as well – all there on Louisette's wedding-
day, well over fifty Paolinos by birth or marriage.

There were, of course, other non-Paolino wedding guests
as well, but with true Paolino hospitality nobody seems to
have dreamed of counting heads. All one knows is that after
the beautiful and most moving marriage ceremony, a hundred
and more of them sat down to an excellent wedding luncheon,
and with all those Paolinos present, every one a gifted and
gay conversationalist, everything went off most happily –
'merry as a marriage bell', as the English saying so aptly puts it.

Now Grand'mère Jenny had been pleased to learn that her
grandson had at last found a girl he wished to marry, indeed,

according to Francis, the only girl he would ever dream of asking to become his wife and share his life. And judging by her photograph and all Grand'mère Jenny heard about Louisette, she certainly sounded very suitable for Francis. And very pretty as well.

However, Grand'mère Jenny was not there at the wedding. She never could be persuaded to travel far from home and she had roundly declared that someone – she herself, of course – had to stay there at Tassin, to keep an eye on everything, and make sure the house was well-aired and warm and in apple-pie order for Francis's bride when she arrived in her new home.

Being Grand'mère Jenny, she wasn't admitting, above all to herself, that a journey down to the Cap d'Antibes in the middle of January, and all the emotion and excitement of the wedding might perhaps be too much for someone of her age. No-one ever dared to comment on Grand'mère Jenny's age, much less tactfully hint that anything might be too much for her. At least, one didn't comment twice – not in front of Grand'mère Jenny.

But naturally, as she bustled round on her grandson's wedding-day, making the house shine like a new pin, and feeding the hens and the rabbits, Grand'mère Jenny's mind went back to other weddings, above all the weddings of her own four children, Antoine, Galmier, Clothilde and Marie. And she remembered with a glow of maternal pride how handsome they had all looked, and how she had presented each of them with a wedding gift of a gold piece. One didn't have bundles of dirty tattered paper money in those days, thought Grand'mère Jenny. One had honest gold, silver and copper coins that looked, and weighed, what they were worth. But how ancient it made one feel now to remember that these fine gold pieces were known by two royal names. One either called them 'louis' after King Louis-Philippe 1st, the 'roi-citoyen', the 'king-citizen' he'd been called, his tastes being all very homely and simple, or one called them 'napoleons' after Napoleon III. Grand'mère Jenny, however, had no opinion whatever of Napoleon III and his disastrous Franco-Prussian War in which her poor man had all but starved, so to her all gold pieces were 'louis'; and she had doggedly saved and saved until she had enough to give each of her four children a gold louis worth twenty francs on their wedding day. Twenty francs made a substantial sum of money in those days.

It always did Grand'mère Jenny good to remember those four gold 'louis', and far better still, those four 'Certificats d'Etudes'. A woman felt she had achieved something in life just to remember all this.

Grand'mère Jenny then wondered again what kind of a wife this pretty young girl was going to make. She was an only child and no doubt spoilt by her parents. But heavens above, hadn't Grand'mère Jenny felt just like this thirty years ago when Antoine first brought Claudia home to Chamboeuf? Claudia, too, had been an only child, and she had made a golden wife and mother, as dear to Grand'mère Jenny as her own four children, a real daughter to her, never, never a daughter-in-law.

Remembering Claudia, Grand'mère Jenny's eyes filled with tears. She had worked so hard; she had been so clever, so full of gaiety, so full of faith and enthusiasm, the life and soul of her home. And she hadn't even lived to see the triumph of her son's first new rose. And now she wasn't there at Antoine's side to see their son married to pretty little Louisette Paolino. A sad pity for Louisette as well. Claudia would have made the best, the kindest of mothers-in-law.

Ah well, the poor child would have to put up with her, Grand'mère Jenny, a 'grandmother-in-law', an impatient outspoken old woman who never sat still herself and never expected anyone else to do so either. Oh yes, Grand'mère Jenny knew her failings even if she saw no sense in admitting them – except occasionally to heaven, of course.

Then Grand'mère Jenny solemnly promised herself, and heaven, always to remember that Louisette was so young; and above all never, never, on any occasion to be tempted to compare her with Claudia – at least not aloud. Claudia would have hated that. She would have wanted her young daughter-in-law to love her. And God forbid that Grand'mère Jenny should ever darken her kind loving memory, even perhaps embitter little Louisette by eternally holding Claudia up to her as an example, a paragon – no matter how sorely tempted Grand'-mère Jenny might well feel in the days to come.

All the same Grand'mère Jenny hoped to heaven she wouldn't be too sorely tempted, and let her tongue gallop away with all these solemn resolutions.

She also hoped to heaven that Louisette wasn't like all these other modern flighty young women, plastering their faces with creams and powders, even painting their lips the most unnatural of scarlets. Grand'mère Jenny didn't hold with all this deceptive 'make-up'. Downright ungodly and unwholesome she always thought it, and a wicked waste of time and money into the bargain. Soap and water, that was all a girl needed to be fresh and attractive.

Grand'mère Jenny then looked down on her old iron hook and decided she'd better wear her fine artificial hand on the day Francis brought his young bride home. Grand'mère Jenny had secretly never seen the necessity for such extravagance but her children had insisted on fitting her up with a splendidly natural-looking artificial hand. She didn't wish to appear ungrateful so she dutifully wore it to Mass every Sunday, and on all red-letter occasions, but she always covered it with a protective black glove. A woman couldn't run risks with so costly an artificial hand; she couldn't give something a carefree whack or bang with it as she could with a stout old iron hook. So Grand'mère Jenny was always very careful and ill-at-ease when wearing that splendid artificial hand; and most thankfully took it off the moment she could. And then with her useful old hook back in its place again, and an apron around her waist, Grand'mère Jenny felt truly at home, and ready to tackle anything.

However, she would, of course, put on that hand to greet Louisette. Later on the child would get used to seeing her with her old iron hook, not even notice it, just like everyone else.

Grand'mère Jenny looked up at the clock and decided the wedding luncheon must now be coming to an end. No doubt there would be somebody on his feet making a speech, making them all laugh, Grand'mère Jenny trusted. One shed enough tears in life as it was. A bride and bridegroom ought to see nothing but happiness all around them on their wedding-day. Yes, she trusted someone was now on his feet and having the kind sense to make everyone laugh.

As it happened, someone *was* on his feet at that moment, and he most certainly was making everyone roar with laughter. It was the bride's father, and he was declaring that here was black ingratitude if one pleased. For years and years, he, Francesco Paolino, had been one of Papa Meilland's best and most faithful customers, always paying his bills bang on the nail. And how does he repay him? Down from Lyons comes this brigand of a son of his, now sitting there smiling with all his white teeth – and carries off his one and only daughter.

The bride's mother dutifully joined in the laughter, of course, but she also swiftly mopped her eyes, remembering again all those kilometres between the Cap d'Antibes and Tassin near

Lyons, such a long way off for a one and only daughter to go and live, especially when the grandchildren came along. Then she looked again at Louisette and Francis and her heart brimmed over; they were both so touchingly, so very much in love.

But she also once again decided that Louisette was the perfect wife for fortunate Francis Meilland, even if it was her own Maman who thought so.

And in this case the bride's mother proved to be absolutely right. Furthermore, the bridegroom's father was thinking precisely the same thing. Yes, there sat Papa Meilland lost in gratitude, thanking the good God that his son had found such a wife. And when he listened again, why another gentleman was now on his feet, proposing yet another toast, and poetically declaring that the lovely young bride was stepping from one world of roses straight into another.

This was literally true – a frequent coincidence in this family story – for presently Louisette and Francis were merrily waved off to spend a fortnight's honeymoon in an idyllic villa among acres of roses, all still in bloom, in Morocco. They had been warmly invited there by a friendly and most hospitable rosegrower.

Grand'mère Jenny would have been considerably taken aback to know that a fortnight later as Louisette sat with Francis in the train taking them home to Tassin, she, too, was making herself, and heaven, the most solemn of promises. Louisette was vowing always to remember Grand'mère Jenny's great age, and that though she might look and sound formidable, she really had a heart of gold and would lay down her life for her family. Louisette was, therefore, always going to be very kind and indulgent to Grand'mère Jenny – no matter how sorely she might be tried in the days to come.

All the same, Louisette fervently hoped she wouldn't be too often sorely tried. In fact, she would always have to keep in mind how well Francis's mother, Claudia, had got on with Grand'mère Jenny. And Louisette had secretly made up her mind to be just like her unknown mother-in-law. A girl couldn't help but be strangely moved by the look in everyone's eyes, the note that came into their voices when they spoke of Claudia. Not only Francis and Papa Meilland, but everyone else who had known her. Everyone.

So Louisette solemnly promised herself, and heaven, to be extra kind, extra tolerant, to Grand'mère Jenny, and never, never wistfully compare her to Francis's mother. At least never aloud. Oh yes, Louisette was going to be the most exemplary of 'grand-daughters-in-law'.

Now Louisette, like any other girl, did a few deft repairs to her 'make up' before they arrived at Tassin. But she was Francesco Paolino's daughter; she had all his delicate 'flair', his sense of colour, and it seems Grand'mère Jenny gave her one anxious look and then most warmly kissed and welcomed her. And never once did she ever seem to notice that Louisette always used a little more than plain soap and water.

But Papa Meilland says that this is what completely won Grand'mère Jenny's old heart – Louisette soon showed she had also inherited all the Paolino courage, not to mention her own little Maman's as well. She made it plain from the very start that she was going to play her full part, not only in Francis's heart, but in all his work as well. She already dearly loved roses, of course, but now she would say, 'Show me how!' and soon she was working at Francis's side as absorbed and dedicated as he was.

Papa Meilland says this didn't astonish him; after all, Louisette *was* Francesco Paolino's daughter. But this moved him beyond words – Louisette also taught herself to type and soon there she was, courageously tackling their ever-growing correspondence, just as Claudia, his own wife, had once done.

But the truth must be told. Life certainly wasn't all roses for Louisette at first. A girl can be deeply in love with her husband, prepared to work at his side, follow him if needs be to the end of the earth, but this doesn't prevent her from missing her gay little Papa and her Maman. Moreover, Louisette also missed the gay sunshine, the warm blue sea and sky of the Cap d'Antibes. Up there at Tassin near Lyons, the sky was so often sober and grey; at times in winter one even had fogs. Admittedly these fogs were not the 'pea-soupers' through which one groped one's frost-bitten way in London – as described by Charles Dickens in the first chapter of a famous novel, one of those 'set books' in France for examination purposes, and through which Louisette and all her class had once shivered their halting way. So maybe Charles Dickens would have pooh-poohed those occasional fogs at Tassin near Lyons, but any fog is very much a fog to a girl from the Cap d'Antibes on the sunny Côte d'Azur.

Francis, of course, was always most understanding and sympathetic. Indeed, he, too, would often think and talk of the Cap d'Antibes and agree how wonderful it would be if one lovely day they could all move down there. But to be honest, Francis wasn't only thinking of Louisette's delight and that of her Papa and Maman, he was also thinking of the new roses he was forever dreaming and working to create. Down there, those delicate, difficult new rose-seedlings would do so much better, grow so much faster, show results so much earlier. And so speed up the work all round.

But one had to be realistic. Times had changed. The land on the Cap was no longer 'a sou a metre' as in Mamma Paolino's days. The Cap had now indeed been 'discovered' – and by wealthy people, sun-lovers, who were building fine villas there. In fact, one grew pale to consider how much it would cost now to buy enough land to establish a rose-garden there, not to mention the huge expense and risk of such an upheaval.

However, as Papa Meilland had already proved for himself more than once, it is always salutary every now and then to follow the advice of that breezy, rollicking English hymn and count one's blessings, 'count them one by one'; and when Francis and Louisette counted up theirs, they gratefully had to acknowledge that they had a great many blessings for a young married couple.

'Meilland and Son' had now achieved a first-class reputation with a growing number of clients all over Europe as well as there in France.

And the name of 'Francis Meilland' was beginning to mean more and more in the world of hybridists. Professional rose-growers, very impressed by the success, the qualities of his first new rose, 'Golden State', were showing the most encouraging interest in any future new rose Francis might now create.

Above all, high above all, they were in love and so happy together.

As for a move to the Cap d'Antibes one day, well, that was just a dream, a delightful but impossible dream. One simply cannot have everything in life.

Papa Meilland says that to understand the next part of their family story one must now 'flash back' to the year 1935 when he had again helped Francis to select fifty of the most promising young seedlings among the offsprings of yet another cross-pollination.

As always, this new family of rose-seedlings had been enormous, at least eight hundred of them; and believe Papa

Meilland, it had again been no simple, easy job to inspect that army and decide on those fifty.

True, it was very agreeable to hear Francis declare, 'Oh, Papa never makes a mistake!' but Papa himself would not care to swear to that. No, indeed. Not when confronted with eight hundred seedlings, every one of them different from the rest.

So it would be far more accurate to say that between them they again decided on fifty and then carefully transplanted them to one of their 'trial beds', each with its identifying label around its frail stem. Francis now had dozens of notebooks in the left-hand drawer of his desk, and one had only to consult the numbers on the little label of any one of their new rose-seedlings, then turn up the right notebook, and there would be a careful record of its parents, grandparents, great-grand-parents, together with the date and order of each cross-pollination. In short, the family-tree of each new little rose-seedling.

They now had several 'trial beds' in the garden, of course, and Francis and Papa Meilland gave them all a regular and careful inspection. But not one of the fifty new rose-seedlings in that particular bed looked in the least outstanding. And certainly the insignificant little one in the far corner, labelled 3 – 35 – 40, looked no more remarkable than the forty-nine others. In fact, it just 'got by' as it were; it was promising enough, that was all. And the following year little 3 – 35 – 40 was 'budded' with the rest of that completely unsensational family of new roses.

Four years later Francis and Papa Meilland were very pleased and proud of the new roses now coming into bloom in their 'trial beds'. And as luck would have it, in June of that year some important national and international conferences of professional rose-growers were held in France. And Francis persuaded Papa Meilland that they ought to invite some of their best clients to spend a day with them at Tassin so that, as Francis himself wrote later on: 'they might share our hopes, and we might show them what we were seeking to achieve'.

Louisette, too, thought this an excellent idea; the new roses that year were truly lovely. But she was only nineteen, she'd only been married six short months, and she would have to be hostess to these important clients, French and foreign, and plan an excellent meal for them, one they would all enjoy.

'Oh, I'll leave everything to you,' said Francis, as confident and carefree as if Louisette was a glittering 'cordon-bleu' with successful years of entertaining important people behind her.

But Papa Meilland says she again showed that she had a real Paolino head on her young shoulders. She most sensibly decided to plan a menu likely to appeal to most men, no matter what their nationality – good plain fare, but all of excellent quality and beautifully cooked. So she spent hours talking food to Grand'mère Jenny who, if you remember, had once been a cook in a fine house. And she spent still more hours with her head deep in that old French classic guide to cooking: 'La Véritable Cuisine de Famille, par Tante Marie'.

And what Tante Marie couldn't tell Louisette, Grand'mère Jenny could, and right willingly did. And Papa Meilland says presently his little daughter-in-law had that menu planned and ready to go into action as efficiently as any Chief Chef preparing a banquet for Monsieur the President of the Republic of France.

From the moment their visitors arrived at Tassin, that day in June was the most heart-warming success. They came from many countries, between them they spoke many languages, but roses in bloom are like music, they need no interpreter, they reach out beyond all barriers of race and language. And every new rose in their 'trial beds' was closely examined and warmly admired.

But queen of them all was a regal new rose with the most handsome buds slowly opening under the warm June sun into glorious, most generous blooms shading from ivory to pale gold and fringed with a delicate pink; and these clear gentle colours seemed to vary from hour to hour, from flower to flower, an enchantment to watch. To add to this glory, the stems were strong and straight, and the handsome dark green leaves had a vigour, a sheen all their own. And the label about its stem said: 3 – 35 – 40.

Yes. It was 3 – 35 – 40, insignificant no longer, that stole the show and every rose-grower's heart.

And it seems these experienced rose-growers looked and looked at the fresh, outstanding glory of 3 – 35 – 40, and admired it more and more, and asked for nothing better, in half a dozen languages, than to try it out at home as soon as supplies of budded stock were available.

It was not, however, only the triumph of 3 – 35 – 40 that made that lovely June day in 1939 so memorable, so poignant to remember in the years to come. There was something in the very air, something most kind and friendly, and they were never to forget how peacefully they sat, talking away, relishing the excellent meal, a triumph of delicious simplicity, so admirably planned by Louisette – with the help of Grand'mère Jenny, of course, and the 'Véritable Cuisine' of Tante Marie. The talk was all of roses, of course, with one rose-grower merrily translating as best he could for another, helping one another out, so that everyone took part in the conversation. And they forgot for that one sunlit day in their peaceful friendliness the dark clouds of war again menacing the world, with Adolf Hitler bellowing non-stop, crescendo, in Germany, and

Mussolini in Italy swaggering away and boasting of most glorious conquests to come.

And the tragedy, the lunacy of it all, thought Papa Meilland, was that the world was full of men like these sitting there around their table at Tassin, men with homes and families, honest hardworking men who would much, much prefer roses to guns.

Neither is Papa Meilland ever likely to forget how, when that merry meal came to an end, it was their German rose-grower friend who rose to his feet and said he knew he spoke for all their visitors when he thanked them for so happy and so interesting a day, and paid them the warmest compliments. Then, face suddenly betraying great emotion, he expressed the heartfelt hope that next year they might again meet under the peaceful blue sky among the roses of Tassin.

But those friendly rose-growers who had so admired 3 – 35 – 40 were not to meet again for many a black year; some of them never. Three months later Hitler's armies roared into Poland, and the Second World War began.

Grand'mère Jenny stood one day in that terrible September of 1939 and looked at the new and costly cold store so optimistically built to shelter rose-bushes in winter. And for the first time in her life she was grateful her poor man was not there, that he had not lived to worry in his old age about this war as well.

Men at the top, decided Grand'mère Jenny, hadn't learnt a thing, not a solitary scrap of sense in all the sixty-nine years since that cruel Franco-Prussian War that had so haunted her poor man.

The First World War, 'to end all wars', seemed only yesterday, not twenty-five years ago, to Grand'mère Jenny, and now, once again, men were being marched off to massacre other men they'd never met, never before set eyes on. No, Grand'-mère Jenny would never understand such wicked folly, not if she lived to be a hundred.

Ah well, one must never lose faith, however. That would be sinful, decided Grandmère Jenny, and no use whatever. One must always hope, pray, and work.

Bitter heart-breaking work it was, too, especially that first winter when Papa Meilland and Francis, helped by a lad of fourteen and an aged gardener, all the staff they had left, had to dig up and burn to ashes two hundred thousand excellent rose-bushes, devastate with their own hands the gardens they had toiled so long and hard to establish.

They would have to grow vegetables now, just as Claudia had done all through the First World War. However, they managed to save enough bushes to keep their business alive, most precariously alive – for who wanted to buy and plant roses that Hitler's jack-booted Army might well trample underfoot? Very few optimists, very, very few.

Then Francis had been turned down by the Army when war broke out. In spite of his amazing spirit and energy, he had never been physically strong. And now, as if to compensate, he worked more feverishly than ever before.

Later on, remembering those war-years, Francis wrote:

'In spite of the enormous difficulties we were experiencing, my father inspired us all with confidence; and by any means we could devise, we tried to keep the business alive, and even to go on with our search for new and better roses.'

Confidence! Papa Meilland says he must certainly have been the world's best actor, then, or poker-player, for he often saw ruin staring them straight in the face. There was the time, for instance, when they hopefully managed to dispatch a consignment of rose-bushes to Turkey, yes, Turkey. Payment was to be made on delivery to an agent there who would find ways and means of getting this badly-needed cash to Tassin. All of which had been highly intricate and devious to arrange, of course.

And what happened? The Germans chose that very time to advance into Yugoslavia and they boarded the trains and slung out all the passengers and goods of no military value. So, out too, of course, went that precious consignment of rose-bushes. Maybe some rose-lover found them lying desolately on the railway-track, picked them up, and who knows, they may now be blooming peacefully in some unknown garden of Yugoslavia. Or maybe they were left to wither and die. All they themselves were ever able to learn was that the Germans had 'intercepted' that consignment, and not one bush ever arrived in Turkey.

Neither did they know what had happened to three other, and infinitely more important, consignments. In the very nick of time, immediately before all normal communications in Europe were cut, they had managed to send off two small parcels of budded 3 - 35 - 40, one to their rose-grower friend in Italy, the other to the one in Germany.

The third consignment had also left France in the very nick of time. At dawn one grey November day they received a most guarded and urgent telephone call from the American Consul in Lyons, a friendly and most generous man and a great rose-lover. But now all he said was a terse:

'I'm about to leave. If you like I can take a small parcel for a friend. Maximum weight: one pound.'

They understood. Within two hours a small parcel of budded 3 - 35 - 40 was rushed to the American Consulate, a one-pound parcel carefully addressed to their American rose-grower friend, Mr. Robert Pyle. And up and away flew that small parcel on the last, the very last Clipper to fly from un-happy France to America.

No need to dwell on the bitter humiliation, the sour smell of treachery and defeat, the long hungry desolate years of that Second World War. Far better say they were so much more fortunate than millions of other families all over the war-torn world. They survived.

Often and often, of course, they would naturally wonder what had happened to those three small consignments of 3 – 35 – 40s. Had they even safely arrived? Or had some Gauleiter in Germany, some Blackshirt in Italy 'intercepted' them and tossed them out to wither and die?

Above all, had that very last Clipper to take flight from France arrived safely in America? Please God, it had. They could not bear to think it might have been shot down in flames, and with it that kindly American who had so gener-ously offered to 'take a small parcel to a friend'.

Papa Meilland says that this is the moment to make it clear that, with all communications cut, none of their foreign rose-grower friends knew that they themselves had decided on the name, the only name, for 3 – 35 – 40. There had been no possibility of discussing it with any of them, of course, no chance to explain. Moreover, there had been none of the usual family discussions, no putting together of heads. They had at once unanimously decided that their beautiful, generous and most dependable new rose must bear the name: 'Madame A. Meilland'.

'Madame A. Meilland', the words that had spelt 'Mother' to Francis when he saw them on the envelopes Papa Meilland had sent from the Western Front in the First World War; 'Madame A. Meilland', the courageous woman who had

pushed a heavy handcart laden with vegetables to sell at market
in all winds and weather, who had toiled so cheerfully and
faithfully by the side of Papa Meilland and their son, loved
them, encouraged them – this was *her* rose.

And when their rose-grower friends in other lands proved
its beauty and enduring qualities – as they would one day,
please God – they would most surely understand and approve.

Presently, however, news trickled through to them that their
friendly German client had not only safely received his small
consignment of 3 – 35 – 40 but, in spite of all difficulties and
crippling restrictions, he had also managed to try it out in his
own garden; and he was so much in love with it that he, too,
had given it a name: Gloria Dei.

And it was being sold under that name in Hitler's Germany.
And Glory be to God, indeed, that he had dared to give it so
significant, so lovely a name, courageously ignoring the 'All
Highest War Lord' now lording it over sullen, hungry, occupied Europe.

Then came still more news; and this trickled through to
them in an equally roundabout way – from Italy this time.
Their rose-grower there had also safely received his small
consignment of 3 – 35 – 40; he, too, had managed to test it,
prove its wonderful qualities, and he had given it the happiest
of Italian names: Gioia! Joy!

This, too, warmed their hearts, for who in their senses would
associate joy with bellowing Duce Mussolini.

But no news whatever came trickling through about that
last Clipper to America, that small one-pound consignment
addressed to Robert Pyle. How could it, they told one another,
with a vast ocean stretching between France and America?
So they hoped and prayed, and worked on.

Presently, their own family life, and thank God for it, too,
became far more lively, and far noisier. Louisette and Francis

became the Maman and Papa of two lovely babies, first a sturdy little boy, Alain, and then a dainty little girl, Michèle. And they, of course, made Papa Meilland and Francesco Paolino the proudest of grandfathers and little Marie-Elisabeth the most delighted of grandmothers.

Michèle and Alain also made Grand'mère Jenny a great-grandmama of course, but would one imagine this to behold her? No, one would NOT. She was still doing the work of two women with her one hand only, helped out with her old iron hook on the other; only deaf as a post when they dared to implore her to consider that a great-grandmama, in all conscience, could sit back, take her ease, and watch the rest of the family carry on with the work.

Sit back! Take her ease! Watch others at work! Not Grand'mère Jenny. And one could not reason with Grand'mère Jenny, not about sacred topics like work. She would have got on famously with that stern seventeenth-century English moralist who, too, considered it was one's bounden duty to 'improve each shining hour'. And she wasn't going to change the habits of a lifetime now, no, not to oblige any mistaken one of them.

One must also be honest, and admit that it would have made *them* feel so much easier seeing her taking a well-earned rest, but it would have made Grand'mère Jenny utterly miserable. So she had her way.

Louisette says she made the most wonderful of great-grandmamas, and that there was something that brought the tears to one's eyes to watch how deftly and gently she would pick up and nurse a fretful baby with her one good hand and the old iron hook on the other, and love and cuddle it close, comfort it just like any other granny.

She dearly loved both her great-grandchildren, but Alain had been born on Grand'mère Jenny's birthday, May 25th, so, to her, he was a very special baby indeed. And all sentiment apart, there was unmistakably a very special bond between Grand'mère Jenny and Alain. As soon as he could crawl and stagger round on his two feet he was always with Grand'mère Jenny. He followed her everywhere.

'He's the image of ME,' Grand'mère Jenny would proudly declare, 'except for the eighty years difference between us.' And off they would go to find wild tasty plants in the hedges to feed to their rabbits, and best of all to Alain, when autumn came, Grand'mère Jenny would use the splendid iron hook on her one arm to pull down the scarlet rose-hips from the wild rose-trees, and give them to him to pile into their basket. Between them, Grand'mère Jenny and little Alain gathered many a kilogramme of wild rose-hips, and Alain would gravely listen as Grand'mère Jenny explained how the tiny seeds inside these rose-hips would all grow into little rose-bushes, wild ones of course, but they would come in most useful one day when the war was over and won.

Grand'mère Jenny, of course, was making quite certain that no time would be wasted after this war as it had been after the First World War when Papa Meilland had to cycle and tramp miles, spend days on end finding and digging up wild rose-trees to make the hardy 'understock' he so desperately needed.

Now to travel anywhere at all in Occupied France was difficult, often absolutely impossible. But at times they managed to get train tickets and take little Alain and Michèle down to the Cap d'Antibes. And it seems they looked at their diminutive grandpapa, Francesco Paolino, and then at their tiny dainty grandmama, Marie-Elisabeth, and decided to call them Pepette and Memette. But again, don't ask anyone why or how, for no-one can tell you. All one knows is that they became Pepette and Memette to Alain and Michèle, and that these names seemed to fit them like a glove, for soon there they were, Pepette and Memette to everyone else as well. Moreover, that is what they still are to this very day.

Now, all through that Second World War Pepette and Memette were also busily growing vegetables, of course, but they, too, managed to keep a small selection of first-class rose-bushes in one corner of their garden. And as Pepette had said years ago in that First World War, don't pity him too much, in fact don't pity him at all. He and Memette had enough to eat, and from time to time, even if it was only at rare intervals, they were able to see Louisette and Francis and Papa Meilland and hug and kiss their two grandchildren. So they were for-tunate beyond words compared with so many millions of other grandparents lost in hungry misery and black sorrow the sad world over.

In December, 1943, it was decided that Papa Meilland, Francis, Louisette and the children ought to take one of these rare trips down to the Cap d'Antibes so that Pepette and Memette might have the pleasure for once of having them all there for Christmas and the New Year. As Grand'mère Jenny herself roundly declared, it might be war-time, but it was also only right and Christian that all grandparents should have their family around them on great feast-days once in a while.

But it was no use whatever trying to persuade Grand'mère Jenny to go with them. She so plainly hated leaving home for more than a day. But that year, 1943, she staggered them all by briskly saying that once she had safely seen them off, once they were no longer 'under her feet', she intended to oblige them all – she would sit down, put up both her feet and have a good rest. So kindly spare her the entreaties not to do too much, to take things quietly and all the rest of their usual little litany. This time she fully intended to take a rest whilst they were away.

Now Grand'mère Jenny, as you must have gathered by now, was always direct and forthright. She believed in plain speaking, and she announced her intention to take a rest in so matter-of-fact a way, as if she did indeed only wish to oblige them, that though they were astonished, and indeed very pleased to think she was going to be so sensible for once, nobody was in the least alarmed.

Not until they came home again. And found Grand'mère Jenny resting in bed. Nobody had ever seen Grand'mère Jenny resting in *bed*, and in broad daylight too, with her one busy old hand lying on the counterpane, so unnaturally still and idle.

Grand'mère Jenny was never again to rise at cock-crow to do the work of two women with her one toil-worn hand. She quietly lay on in her bed, entrusted her soul to the good God who understands us all, thanked Him most gratefully she could now leave Claudia's 'two men' to kind Louisette, and most peacefully went to her eternal rest. She was eighty-seven, but she had never once, till then, permitted anyone to remember this.

They all missed her terribly, of course. As Louisette says, the world would be a saner better place if there was a Grand'mère Jenny in every family. As for Papa Meilland, he may be over eighty himself now, but the tears still come to his eyes to remember so good and valiant a mother, and he still exclaims:

'But when one thinks of it! The first time she took a rest – it was the death of her.'

That same year, 1943, rumours were already beginning to spread like wild-fire in France that in spite of all Hitler's bellowing fury, his demented orders to stay put, freeze, and die fighting like heroes, the German Army was falling back and back in Russia, losing two million men as they retreated, frozen, killed, or prisoners of war. And all the propaganda blaring nonstop from the Nazi-controlled radio could not smother, stamp out the truth.

Then it came – the long-awaited day. On June 6th, 1944, the Allies at last landed on the coast of Normandy; and all France held its breath as they began to drive the German Army, fighting most desperately, back and back towards the Rhine.

In August, mysterious radio messages began to be repeated again and again on certain wave-lengths:

'This buzzing makes one dizzy.'

'Nancy has a crick in her neck.'

'Gaby is going to lie down on the grass.'

Hearing these sibylline messages, the local F.F.I. – the secret Resistance Army of Southern France – immediately stepped up their incessant guerilla-warfare against the Germans, ruthlessly sabotaging anything and everything that might be of any immediate military use to them – roads, railway-lines, bridges, telegraph posts, everything, until everyday life ground to a tense, expectant standstill. Only the cicadas sang on and on under the hot August sun; indeed, one would have sworn they, too, were relentlessly repeating, 'this buzzing makes one dizzy', 'Nancy has a crick . . . crick . . . crick in her neck – neck – neck.'

And when night fell on August 14th, out from certain ports of liberated Italy and North Africa sailed twenty-six ships laden with troops and equipment – a Free French and American Army under the command of General de Lattre, every ship making straight for the beaches between Calvaire and Saint Tropez on the south coast of France.

Papa Meilland says the air immediately became charged with wild and conflicting rumours, but presently two truths emerged

crystal clear: that long-awaited Army of Liberation had success-
fully landed on those beaches and was now on its way up the
valley of the River Rhône towards Lyons with the Germans
ferociously fighting back, but steadily retreating.

Most welcome news, of course, but Louisette was white,
frozen, with anguish. One of these 'well-informed' people who
always claim to have vital secret information denied to the
rest of us swore that the Cap d'Antibes and the little town of
Antibes as well, were blazing from end to end, not a roof
was left on any house, hardly a soul there could still be
alive.

None of this was official, of course. How could it be? Not
a train was running; not a card, a letter, a telegram, a telephone
message was possible. And Papa Meilland says that Francis,
face grim and set, decided there was only one thing to do –
go down to the Cap and see for himself, and if they were still
alive, somehow, some way he would bring Pepette and
Memette back to Tassin with him. And he grabbed his bicycle,
stuffed some food in his saddle-bag, and set off.

He made straight for the Route Nationale 7, the great road
that runs from Paris to Lyons and then on to the Riviera; and
as he pedalled furiously along, he prayed his worn tyres might
last out, and above all that he and his bicycle might get an
occasional lift on one of the American Army trucks that were
now said to be running to and fro, 'faisant la navette' as the
French put it, between villages and towns as fast as they were
liberated.

Both his prayers were answered. From time to time he was
able to sling his bicycle on one of those American trucks, and
the driver would clap an American helmet firmly on his French
head, and he'd do his best to keep well out of sight and try to
look American, and presently 'beat it' with his bicycle, as
agreed, just before the American truck made its official halt

at some village or town. And many, many a time did Francis
thank heaven that he had learnt English, that he had once
talked his way around America, for now he was able to explain
why he was in such a hurry to get down to the Cap d'Antibes
and to express his gratitude to those sympathetic American
truck-drivers.

His tyres also mercifully held out, and when he at last came
pedalling into Antibes, not a house lay in ruins, all the gay
red tiles were still on the roofs, and out there on the Cap, the
sun shone down on the peaceful gardens, the villas, and there
it stood, not a window shattered, the house of Pepette and
Memette. And there were Pepette and Memette, safe and
sound; and there he was, speechless with relief, and grey with
dust and sudden exhaustion.

Memette wasted no time. She immediately set a meal before
him, made him eat, and packed him straight off to bed. And
twenty-four hours later, he was back on Route Nationale 7,
again pedalling furiously, or yelling out, and again getting an
occasional lift from any passing, and sympathetic American
truck-driver. By the end of the week, he came pedalling back
to Tassin, and almost fell off his bicycle. There was no need
for words, Louisette saw the look on his face, and burst into
tears – tears of dear relief and most poignant and loving
gratitude.

By the end of that momentous feverish month of August,
the Parisians went singing and weeping for joy along their
boulevards. Their city, the heart of France, was free again.
And presently the whole of France was set free as well, and
Germany herself was tasting invasion, by the Russians to the
East, and by the Americans, the British, and the French to the
West.

A month to the day after the Liberation of France, a letter

arrived at Tassin, a letter with an American stamp. Hands shaking with excitement, Francis tore it open, and then stood very still and silent, looking down at it.

'Well . . . ?' breathed Louisette.

'Yes,' said Francis. 'It is. It is from him. From Mr. Robert Pyle.'

CHAPTER TWELVE

'Peace'

It seems one would need to be a Shakespeare or Victor Hugo to pin down in words how they felt when Francis translated and read aloud that first post-war letter from America. All they could say at first was, 'Ah, no! Read it again. Slowly this time.'

Then Francis would slowly and carefully translate every word as if he too was struggling to assure himself that all he was reading was true, that this was, indeed, a letter from Robert Pyle of Pennsylvania, America.

But there in black and white were the friendly greetings and a whole catalogue of facts, figures, and dates that read like beautiful fiction. And there, too, was the signature, the unmistakably bold and generous signature:

Robert Pyle.

'Whilst dictating this letter,' he wrote, 'my eyes are fixed in fascinated admiration on a glorious rose, its pale gold, cream and ivory petals blending to a lightly ruffled edge of delicate carmine.

'There it is before me, majestic, full of promise, and I am convinced it will be the greatest rose of the century.'

Robert Pyle was singing the praises of 3 – 35 – 40. Their prayers had been answered. That last Clipper to leave Occupied France for America had safely arrived; that generous American had kept his promise; Robert Pyle had received that hastily-packed one-pound consignment of 3 – 35 – 40.

And Robert Pyle had wasted no time; he had at once set to work. He had not only promptly propagated 3 – 35 – 40, planted it out and tested it in his own 'trial beds', he had also sent supplies to be tested by many other eminent professional rose-growers with gardens up and down the United States of America. In short, it had been most rigorously tested in all manner of American soils, in all kinds of American weather, from the hot dry rose-fields of Texas to the cool damp fields of Michigan. And in every rose-field it had been a glorious success; it had won the hearts of all rose-growers everywhere.

It seemed they had been delighted to observe that the bush itself was as remarkable as the lovely roses it bore; it was so hardy, vigorous, and resistant to any treacherous late spring frosts.

Two other qualities of 3 – 35 – 40 had also impressed those American rose-growers: the beautiful buds seemed to open more slowly than those of other roses; and the fully-opened blooms were not only long-lasting, they also kept all the delicate freshness of the half-open buds.

The American Rose Society had then studied the reports sent in by their members who between them represented every state in America, and they had been so assured of the exceptional qualities of 3 – 35 – 40 that they decided to pay the warmest of tributes to this outstanding new rose that had literally arrived out of the blue from desolate, enemy-occupied France.

They agreed to organise a 'Name Giving Ceremony' for it at the Pacific Rose Society's Exhibition at Pasadena, California, on Sunday, April 29, 1945. This date, of course, had to be decided upon many months in advance.

The war was still raging in Europe, communications were still cut, and there was no way of knowing if Papa Meilland

and Francis were still alive, or if their rose-gardens at Tassin near Lyons still existed. Robert Pyle had therefore consulted other eminent professional rose-growers, and between them they had drawn up this moving statement:

'We are persuaded that this greatest new rose of our time should be named for the world's greatest desire: PEACE.

'We believe that this rose is destined to live on as a classic in our grandchildren's gardens and for generations to come. We would use the word "Peace" to preserve the knowledge that we have gained the hard way that Peace is increasingly essential to all mankind, to be treasured with greater wisdom, watchfulness, and foresight than the human race has so far been able to maintain for any great length of time.

'Towards that end, with our hopes for the future, we dedicate this lovely new rose to:

'PEACE.'

And on that sunny Sunday, April 29, 1945, before a great gathering of rose-lovers who had travelled to Pasadena from all over America, two white doves were set free and soared high into the blue Californian sky as 3 – 35 – 40 was solemnly given its lovely American name, 'Peace'.

And call it singular coincidence or what you will, but on that day, fixed so long in advance, Berlin fell.

Robert Pyle then wound up his letter by saying how much he was hoping and praying it would safely reach them, and how warmly delighted he would now be to have news of them, *good* news; and meanwhile he was always theirs very sincerely,

Robert Pyle.

Papa Meilland says that never before could there have been a more welcome and friendly letter from America. But all he himself could do was get up abruptly, go down to the cellar, and bring up a hidden bottle and pour them all a festive and steadying little glass; and they drank to Peace and Freedom, and Robert Pyle and all other rose-lovers the wide world over.

All in one grateful toast – but in that order, Peace and Freedom first.

That night Francis took his pen and strove to find words to set down all that was in their hearts.

'Fate has willed,' he wrote, 'that our rose, 3 – 35 – 40, should be known under different names in different countries, but each of these names surely shows that in seeing so lovely a rose, men of good will will cry "Gloria Dei", be moved to "Joy" and will most truly desire "Peace".

'And here, in France, our rose will bloom to the lovely memory of a beloved wife and mother: Madame A. Meilland.'

'Madame A. Meilland', 'Joy', 'Gloria Dei', 'Peace', golden names every one, but this is certain, Claudia herself would have thought that 'Peace' transcended them all.

This welcome post-war letter was the first of many that now came fast one after the other. Imagine how they felt, for instance, to learn that when the forty-nine delegates to the newly-formed United Nations first met in San Francisco, as each delegate came into the hotel room reserved for him, he saw in a vase on a table a beautiful rose with this message before it from the secretary of the American Rose Society:

'This is the rose "Peace" which received its name the day Berlin fell. May it help to move all men of goodwill to strive for Peace on Earth for all mankind.'

On that day, that very day, a truce was declared in devastated Europe. On that day, for the first time in six long cruel years, no bombs fell, the guns were silent; and that night no sirens wailed and the children of Europe slept in peace.

Then came another memorable day when the most critical and discerning of American judges of roses gave the All-American Award to the new rose: 'Peace'.

'Peace'

On that day, the war in Japan came to an end.

A month later, for the very first time in its history, the American Rose Society gave its supreme award, its gold medal, to a new rose. The rose was 'Peace', and on that day a peace treaty was signed in Japan.

Superb American timing? Impossible, for the dates of all famous rose-shows are always fixed months in advance.

Then might it perhaps have been the warm welcome note struck by the very name of the lovely new rose? Again no; for no eminent judge would permit a name to colour his judgment, to lay an axe to his trained impartial appraisal of any rose. And bear in mind this was no all-American rose, it had been created in France, by a Frenchman.

So cry remarkable coincidence or what one may, but here again the truth was far more amazing, far more moving than any far-fetched feat of fiction.

Just as rewarding and even more heart-warming than all the medals, the awards, were the letters that now began to pour in from all parts of the world. It was as if people every-where, utterly sick and weary of brutality, violence, senseless destruction, felt their hearts lift again to see so lovely and generous a rose with so kind and welcome a name.

Again and again they were moved to learn that 'Peace' roses were being planted on many a grave from the Philippines to devastated Rotterdam; that the world over, beds of 'Peace' roses were blooming around hospitals, and in public parks and gardens where old people sit in the sun and children play. One would hardly plant a rose in such quiet unremarkable places because it had become all the rage, or because of its gentle name.

No, maybe the English naturalist, Richard Jefferies, had put a sensitive finger on a great truth when he wrote: 'The hours when the soul is absorbed by beauty are the only hours when we truly live.' For six endless years, hideous destruction and death had had their savage fling, and now just to stand for a moment absorbed, caught up in the tranquil beauty of a new rose, perhaps one caught again a glimpse of what it was to live again, truly live.

Maybe this was why the 'Peace' rose had such a way of winning hearts, making friends wherever it went, as much at home in a cottage garden as in some formal parterre of a palatial estate.

Maybe, too, it was because there was something so generous and dependable about it, something so courageous. After some sudden heavy downpour, for instance, when a garden-lover's heart sinks into his boots to see his other roses so forlornly battered and drooping, there will be 'Peace', in the words of the old sentimental song, still 'smiling through', as courageous as the wife and mother after whom it was first named. And this is not one of those facile florid tributes, far too often paid to the memory of the dead. Ask anyone who knew her and they will tell you that never has any rose come so close to its namesake, that this generous dependable rose has all the lovely qualities of Claudia, Madame A. Meilland, herself.

And nine years after the Americans gave it its lovely name, it was estimated that thirty million 'Peace' rose-bushes were flowering all over the world; and Francis wrote in his diary:

'How rewarding it is for an ordinary working gardener to know his rose is growing in cottage-gardens, in the grounds of mansions, around churches, and mosques and hospitals, and in public parks; and to think that so many people are now seeing the rose he alone once saw in his mind as he strove to create it.

'How strange to think, too, that all these millions of rose-bushes sprang from one tiny seed no bigger than the head of a pin, a seed which we might so easily have overlooked, or neglected in a moment of inattention, or which might have been relished as a tit-bit by some hungry field-mouse. Or even if it had been spared to grow into a tiny fragile seedling, it might so easily have been destroyed by some sudden frost, or some ravenous insect.'

One could argue, of course, that this is the eternal miracle of the survival of all living things, but surely the survival and triumph of 3 – 35 – 40 also owes much to the dear love of roses, the faith in the future, and the hard dedicated work, not only of Francis Meilland himself, but of everyone else in this family story.

But what was now happening to the rose-growers themselves?

Up there at Tassin, near Lyons, every day was full to over-flowing for they now had to restore and restock their gardens, replacing all the thousands of rose-bushes that had gone up in smoke during the war. But the struggle to get going again after this war was very different from the bleak hard fight after the First World War. There was no need for Papa Meilland and Francis to get on battered old bicycles and cycle miles, searching, and digging up wild roses for 'understock' in the forests and hedges.

3 – 35 – 40 had become the most generous of fairy-god-mothers. Money from the stupendous sale of so many 'Peace' roses was flowing in fast, but the vast majority came from America, of course. Robert Pyle had promptly patented 'Peace', and as creators of the new rose, they were receiving a just percentage of the sale of every bush in America.

In every other country, of course, it was a very different story. Professional rose-growers were free as air to buy twenty or so bushes and then themselves go on propagating 'Peace' by the thousands, and never pay a cent more to Francis, no matter how great and profitable their sales.

And Francis swore to himself that one day, God willing, he would find the time, the legal knowledge, to fight this injustice, not for himself alone – he had been fortunate indeed – but for hybridists everywhere, the patient creators of all lovely new flowers and plants.

Meanwhile he and Papa Meilland and Louisette gave grateful thanks for the dollars now rolling in from America as they worked long hours to get the business going again.

All the while, of course, Alain and Michèle were growing so fast that it seemed no time at all to Papa Meilland before he was teaching his grandson to use the eyes the good God had given him just as he had once taught his own son, and just as good Madame Mivière had once taught him in her garden and out in the fields and forests around quiet Chamboeuf. And by the time he was seven, there was never any need to cry, 'But where *is* that boy?' They would know just where to find Alain, either following close behind his Papa or Papa Meilland, intently watching them, asking a thousand questions, or else he would be in his own little garden among his own rose-bushes, happy as a king.

There was never any question of 'what will he do in life?' Alain's young heart was already firmly set on roses, nothing but roses, just like his Papa, just like his two grandpapas – Papa Meilland up there at Tassin and Pepette down there on the Cap d'Antibes, just like his great-grandpapa, Francis Dubreuil and . . . heavens, how time flies! . . . just like his great-great-grandpapa, that good honest gardener, Joseph Rambaux, of the Tête d'Or Park in Lyons.

As for little Michèle, she played at being a florist, cutting and bunching roses for sale to imaginary and splendid clients – clients like stately Madame Rondel of the Ironing Establishment of Grasse or kind Madame la Baronne Alice de Rothschild who, day in day out, wore blouses the colour of old gold and only went out when it rained – as in the stories told by Memette of the days when she herself was young, years and years and years ago. Or so it seemed, of course, to little Michèle. But not, most certainly not to Memette herself. To her, those days seemed only yesterday.

And now she and Pepette, too, were as busy as ever among the roses they were again growing in their gardens and green-houses, cutting and bunching them for sale to their faithful and satisfied clients. But in all his free time Pepette was also still going on with his own search for a new and even more admirable rose, still hoping to cry, 'Stupendo! Magnifico!' one day before a real Paolino paragon of a rose, with stems long and straight as his arm, one that would obligingly keep sweet and fresh for days on end even in the warmest of rooms – the perfect rose for florists to sell to people without gardens.

Oh yes, they were busy, and the days flew by, but naturally they often wished they could see more of their grandchildren. As Memette said, it had been bewildering enough the way their own Louisette shot up, fell in love, and was married, all at the gallop; and the years always seem to whisk by far faster when one became a grandparent; and mark her words, the day after to-morrow, or so it would seem to them, there would be those two grandchildren of theirs grown up, too, and talking of marriage. And they would have seen so little of them as children, so very little.

Up there at Tassin near Lyons, especially on a bleak, rain-swept day, Francis would often fervently agree with Louisette that it would be wonderful to have rose-gardens down there on the Cap where the weather would be so much kinder to delicate little rose-seedlings. And Louisette would also natur-ally think how wonderful it would be to be able to run in and say good-day and kiss Pepette and Memette without first sitting six tedious hours in a train with Alain and Michèle incessantly demanding to know if they were there now. And if not, why not? And what was the matter with this train, crawling along like a snail?

It was not, however, these excellent reasons of head and heart that in 1947 made them begin to consider in all seriousness a move to the Cap d'Antibes only two crowded busy years after the arrival of that momentous letter from America.

Absurd as it sounds, it was because everything was going so very well up there at Tassin!

It was becoming clearer and clearer that they would have to make a major, a vital decision, indeed the greatest decision of their lives. Either they would have to devote all their time and energy and experience to growing first-class rose-bushes for sale – this side of their business was booming – or they would have to devote all their time and skill to their search for new varieties of roses to put on the market. This, too, was rapidly growing in importance. Rose-growers all over the world were now eager to buy any new rose created, tested, and proved by Meilland and Son.

As matters stood, they were in grave danger of falling between two stools. They could no longer do full justice to one without neglecting the other. Which should it be?

But better cut short the long family discussions, the searchings of the heart, the sober warnings of commonsense and prudence, and simply say that up shot the flame, the passionate longing to create new and lovelier roses that Francis's great-grandfather, his grandfather and Papa Meilland himself had known so well; and presently swept all before it.

And very dramatic and risky this seemed to many of their well-meaning friends and neighbours! In fact, Papa Meilland says one could positively hear them darkly thinking, not for the first time, that Francis would most certainly end up now by 'putting his father and all his family on the straw'. And there was a pitying look in their eyes that implied that all these American dollars must have softened poor Papa Meilland's hard head as well.

However, having made the great decision, they at once approached one of their competitors, Monsieur Francisque Richardier, who also had important rose-gardens near Lyons, a man and a rose-grower for whom Papa Meilland had always had the highest regard, and though he says so himself, Papa Meilland is no mean judge of both men and roses.

They therefore called on Monsieur Richardier, and asked if he would be interested in buying their prospering rose-growing business at Tassin, lock, stock and barrel; and proceeded to produce all the necessary facts and figures.

It seems Monsieur Richardier listened in attentive silence to all they had to say, and then that excellent man soberly said:

'If this business of yours is half as good as it sounds, I am astonished you do not wish to retain half of it for your-selves.'

Astonished! It was now Papa Meilland and Francis who were astonished. The idea of retaining a prudent fifty per cent share of the business at Tassin had not even occurred to them, and now the more they considered it, the more sensible, indeed providential, it grew.

So they let no grass grow under their feet. Agreement was soon reached, and with admirable speed and efficiency Monsieur Richardier took over. And up went a new sign, and the rose-gardens at Tassin near Lyons became the 'Etablissement Meilland-Richardier'.

Papa Meilland, taking a last look round, and thinking of the past, was suddenly strangely comforted as if he knew most surely that Claudia would have warmly approved of their bold plan. She was always so eager, so enterprising, so full of new ideas, so full of faith.

Above all, it filled Papa Meilland with the most poignant emotion to think they were bound for the very place Claudia herself had so longed to see. It was as if this, too, was a dream to be realised, fulfilled in her son. And in him.

And suddenly, too, he knew that it had not only been anxiety, fear of the future, that had been nagging away so at the back of his mind. No, no. It had been the feeling that it smacked of near-treachery, lack of all heart, to abandon totally these rose-gardens so full of memories. And Papa Meilland looked up at that new sign: 'Meilland-Richardier', and felt better. Much better.

On the first day of the merry month of May, 1948, Mcmette rolled up her sleeves to prepare the finest 'pasta-asciutta' of her life, and Pepette cut and most artistically arranged the finest of his roses to set on the table, to welcome Papa Meilland, Francis, Louisette and the children to their new home, their new gardens and greenhouses down there on the Cap d'Antibes. Louisette's dream, once so wildly impossible, so impossibly expensive to realise, had come true.

But this costly move was not done with one easy wave of the cheque-book, of course. It, too, was truly part of the miracle of 3 – 35 – 40. All the bills, and some of them made Papa Meilland's hair stand on end, were met with the dollars still flowing in from America. In fact, it was overwhelming, staggering, to think all this had been made possible by such splendid American justice to a rose-grower in far-away France.

Looking back now, Papa Meilland can see that it was their own good fortune that now fanned into even fiercer flame the ideal Francis had so long had in his mind – justice like this for all hybridists everywhere, for all creators of a new and lovely variety of flower or plant.

And the following year, in spite of the heavy incessant work the move had created, Francis still found time to stagger every commercial rose-grower in France. He also staggered Monsieur the Director of Industrial Property up there in Paris.

Monsieur the Director of Industrial Property, you must understand, was, and still is, the only authority in France to whom one can apply for a 'brevet d'invention' – a patent on any invention. And here now was Francis Meilland, a rose-grower, applying for a patent on a new rose he had just created: 'Rouge Meilland', as if this 'Rouge Meilland' were some new tool, some new labour-saving gadget, some new piece of machinery.

Moreover, this rose-grower had engaged an able lawyer, an expert who specialised in the French laws governing the granting of patents. And they proceeded to set convincing evidence, all manner of data, before Monsieur the Director of Industrial Property, all of which proved without a shadow of doubt that Francis Meilland was, indeed, the creator of 'Rouge Meilland', a completely new rose, the only rose of its kind in the world. And that he, therefore, had every legal right to ask for a patent that would give him and his new creation the same protection under the laws of France as the honest creator of any other completely new and unique invention.

Monsieur the Director of Industrial Property, plainly astounded at so unheard of a claim, examined all the evidence and recognised the justice of their claim. And for the first time in all the legal history of France a rose-grower was granted a 'brevet d'invention' for a new rose.

Now the cold truth must be told. As the French adage says: 'There is always another side to every medal.' This triumph also made Francis many enemies. Commercial rose-growers all over France were outraged, positively blazing with indignation.

This patent dynamited, blew sky-high, all age-old custom; and Francis was never to forget how, soon afterwards, he and Monsieur Richardier went to a Horticulturist Congress in Biarritz – a most stormy and contentious congress.

'We both came away profoundly saddened and demoralised,' wrote Francis later on. 'Our good friends of yesterday had been transformed into bitter enemies; enemies because they would not admit the justice of granting a patent for a new variety of plant or flower; they would not admit that one no longer had every right to multiply and sell any new variety as freely as one wished, as freely as one had always done in the past – not once that new variety was granted a patent.'

But hybridists all over France sent up a most grateful 'Te Deum'. Francis Meilland had had the moral courage to take 'le premier pas qui coûte', the first and most difficult of all steps, the one that had always before been considered absolutely impossible. From this victory on, if any hybridist succeeded in creating a new variety of plant or flower, he, too, became as fortunate overnight as any other inventor. He, too, could now apply for a 'brevet d'invention' and so be legally entitled to his fair share of the rewards of his labour.

Now 'Rouge Meilland' was admittedly a bleak and most factual name for a new and beautiful red rose, but Francis felt one ought to be austerely matter-of-fact, not poetically imaginative, when first confronting Monsieur the Director of Industrial Property. Once again, however, their American friends delighted them; they decided on the very name for 'Rouge Meilland'; they called it 'Happiness'. And that just about sums up all they felt when Francis successfully won that first battle in his fight for justice to hybridists, a fight he swore never to abandon, no matter what the opposition, no matter what the cost, until justice was done to all hybridists in every civilised land under the sun.

But justice for hybridists was not all that now blazed so fiercely in Francis's mind. He was one of the rarest of men – a practical visionary. He saw so clearly that a new rose is like a new poem, a new symphony, any new work of art – it is only of lasting value if something about it moves the heart, if it adds something to the beauty, the grace, the all too rare joys of everyday life.

So he wholeheartedly agreed with Papa Meilland, who as always had both his sober feet firmly on the ground, that as they worked to create new roses, they must always keep in mind not the fortunate few with idyllic gardens and the time and money to coddle and coax some exotic but exacting novelty, but the millions of the rest of us who love to buy and plant a new rose-bush as best and where we may. Or having no garden of our own, love to buy roses to mark some red-letter date dear to our hearts.

And Francis now clearly saw the only practical way to translate all their ideals into practical reality. He saw their new rose-gardens and greenhouses on the Cap d'Antibes as the centre of an organisation of first-class rose-growers, a truly international organisation. Between them, they would have gardens all over the world.

There on the Cap they themselves would devote all their time and resources to the creation of new, better, and lovelier roses. They would build still more greenhouses where delicate new rose-seedlings would grow under ideal conditions. In this way the long slow process of selection and cross-pollination would definitely be speeded up.

Only the most promising of new roses would then be taken from the shelter of the greenhouses and planted outside, not only in their own gardens down there on the Cap d'Antibes, but also up there, under the cooler sky, the more exacting climate of the Meilland-Richardier gardens at Tassin near Lyons.

There they would be left to grow and bloom for several years with Monsieur Richardier, Papa Meilland, and Francis keeping a vigilant eye on them. Only when they were satisfied that here was a truly promising new rose would consignments of it be sent to the other members of this organisation.

This would not be the last word, however. Each rose-grower in the organisation would then plant the new rose in a 'trial-bed' in his own home garden, under his own sky, observe it closely, and not for one spring and summer alone, but for three years at least before it was finally agreed that this was, indeed, a new rose they could all confidently include in their catalogues and offer for world-wide sale. Or that here was a new rose they must write off – in spite of all early promise it had finally failed to come up to their high standards.

Francis saw the members of this international organisation meeting every year towards the end of the month of May on the Cap d'Antibes, so that they might see for themselves all Francis and Papa Meilland had that year achieved. Together they would then discuss the progress, or failure, of their new roses, plan ahead for the future, making certain that they kept on the right road.

'We must travel,' wrote Francis, 'we must keep in touch with great horticulturists, with people with small gardens. We must always be on the alert to anything that will help us to know what people everywhere most wish to see in a new rose. Our one goal must always be to assure greater pleasure, greater satisfaction, to anyone who plants a rose-bush or buys a rose from a florist.'

Obviously an international organisation like this, every member an eminent rose-grower, cannot be brought about by a polite exchange of letters. And Papa Meilland was often to remember again that long-ago evening when Francis had set off to join the English Language and Literature Class in Lyons, and how he had suddenly turned in the doorway.

'Do you know,' he had said, 'I now think that one day I shall travel round the world.'

And this from a lad who hadn't even been as far as Paris!

Yet this was precisely what he now did, and at whirlwind speed, white-hot with enthusiasm, ablaze with enthusiastic faith in the future. To Italy, Morocco, Switzerland, England, Spain, Algeria, Belgium, Holland, Germany, Canada, the United States and Mexico he flew in turn, meeting famous rose-growers everywhere, discussing the principles on which their organisation must be based, agreeing on a set of rules to be observed by them all. And between these 'voyages-éclair' (lightning trips), as Papa Meilland called them, Francis would put in long days of hard work in the greenhouses and gardens.

Many a time Papa Meilland thanked God that Louisette understood Francis so well, that she shared all his hopes, his vision, his plans for the future. Otherwise everything might well have gone sour. But theirs was surely the perfect marriage. Louisette loved and cared for them all, she was eternally busy in their new house, the gardens and greenhouses, or tapping away on a typewriter helping to keep pace with all their international correspondence. Best of all, Louisette was like Memette, her own little mother, like Claudia, the mother-in-law she had never known. She, too, knew how to make a real home about her, a friendly and welcoming place for all who came to see them.

As for Alain and Michèle, the Cap d'Antibes was heaven itself to them: the gay sunshine, the warm blue sea, the gardens, and Memette and Pepette only ten minutes away to spoil them outrageously and tell them stories of their great-grandmama Paolino, and Papa the Corporal and Pepette's cric-crac-ing shoes and boots, and the infamous dog, Perla, who had turned up her nose at Memette's first 'pasta-asciutta'.

And it did Papa Meilland's grandfatherly heart good to see how brown and well they looked; and to note how observant and deft Alain was becoming, a born young rose-grower if ever there was one.

One triumphant day in June, 1950, only two years after the great move to the Cap d'Antibes, eighteen of the major rose-growers from eighteen different countries sat around the long table on the shady terrace outside their new house. Beyond the rose-gardens sparkled the sea, the sky overhead was blue and cloudless as those eighteen rose-growers lifted their glasses and drank to 'Universal Rose Selection', the first international organisation for the creation and distribution of new roses.

Another dream had become reality. There, now, sat the members of the organisation Francis had laboured so hard to create, every man pledged 'to assure greater satisfaction to anyone who plants a new rose-bush or buys a rose from a florist'.

Papa Meilland, sitting there with them, still cannot think why, but it was at this moment that his thoughts chose to go back a whole century, to 1850, when that homely gardener, Joseph Rambaux, worked twelve hours a day in the Tête d'Or Park of Lyons, and then came home to devote every moment left of daylight to the roses he so dearly loved to grow in his own small garden; and even found the time, the patience, to create ten beautiful new roses of his own as well.

And here now, on the Cap d'Antibes, one hundred years later, sat Joseph's great-grandson, Francis Meilland, the founder of this unique organisation: 'Universal Rose Selection'.

Then Papa Meilland's wandering thoughts chose to recall

the hard times, the struggles, the frustrations, so many black moments in the past. And his conscience said, 'Well . . . ?' very accusing and reproachful. So Papa Meilland faced up to his conscience and repentantly acknowledged that faith can indeed move mountains; and that he, himself, heaven forgive him, had so often doubted this. Ah well, one lived and learned.

And one worked, too, of course. Saint James knew this. 'Faith without works is dead', that sensible saint had declared. Monsieur the good Curé of Chamboeuf had always drummed that well and truly into the young heads of his Catechism Class. And there now, on that triumphant June day, so many years later, sat Papa Meilland remembering all this.

And as Papa Meilland raised his glass with the others, he felt the good saint would have cheerfully raised a celestial glass with him, not in the least outraged to be taken so literally by a hardworking old rose-grower.

That same year, 1950, a new rose came on the market and quietly became a faithful friend to many a garden-lover in many a land. It had something about it that French rose-catalogues sonorously call 'épanouissement généreux et vigoureux' which, if one seeks the plain truth behind words, means that it settles down with no fuss whatever and gets on with the honest job of growing into a generous and dependable bush.

It is also very upright, and the clear yellow pointed buds have no drooping nonsense about them. They grow erect and determined among the clean shining foliage and open into generous blooms with pale gold petals shading into that lovely deep pink one sometimes sees in homely nasturtiums in a cottage garden; and its scent is very fresh and sweet and clean.

The name of that rose is 'Grand'mère Jenny'. You may well have a bush in your own garden, or you may now come across one in a friend's garden or in a public park. As you pause to admire it, think for a moment of upright Grand'mère Jenny, who did the work of two women with her one good hand and who long years ago worked so valiantly to keep her four children at the little school in the French village of Chamboeuf until they were twelve. And who was so very proud and happy when all four in turn brought home their 'Certificat d'Etudes' to frame and hang on the wall where everyone would see and admire them.

Little did Grand'mère Jenny dream that one day a lovely sweet-smelling rose would be dedicated to her memory; and that it would go straight on to win two splendid Certificates of Honour and two fine gold medals all in one year at four of the greatest international rose-shows.

But, as Papa Meilland says, one can't help feeling that Grand'-mère Jenny herself would be infinitely prouder to know that one still recalls those four 'Certificats d'Etudes' that once hung side by side in pride of place on the living-room wall of a small farm in the quiet and unremarkable French village of Chamboeuf.

CHAPTER THIRTEEN

'Whenever One Thinks of Roses'

From now on, every post began to bring Francis invitations 'from all sides', as Francis himself wrote, 'invitations to attend the formal openings of municipal rose-gardens, or international conferences of professional rose-growers, or meetings of hybridists from all over the world'.

It was impossible to accept many of these invitations, of course, but in spite of the hard work and heavy responsibility on his hands, Francis did his best to accept when he could. He dearly loved to meet and talk to anyone who truly cared about roses. But no planned meeting, no formal professional occasion, ever gave him more pleasure than a chance encounter – in an American Income Tax Office of all unlikely places!

Louisette says Francis had flown off to the States on one of his 'voyages éclair' as Papa Meilland always chose to call them, truly 'lightning trips', when Francis would be busy with them among the roses down there on the Cap d'Antibes one morning, and on the evening of the following day he would be walking and talking hundreds of miles away among the roses of one of their friends of Universal Rose Selection, maybe even on the other side of the world. And twenty-four hours later, sometimes less, there he would be, home and hard at it again among the roses on the Cap d'Antibes; and describing his latest 'lightning trip' so vividly that they always felt they, too, were seeing and hearing all Francis had seen and heard only yesterday – so many miles away.

All of which often made Papa Meilland declare that this modern whirlwind flying around the globe might be time-saving, he wasn't denying that, but it had a disconcerting way of making the world seem altogether different, positively reducing it to pocket-size compared with the vast imposing universe he had always been led to imagine when he was a lad.

Now, on the last afternoon of that particular 'lightning trip', Francis had to pay an obligatory visit to an office in Lexington Avenue in New York, the 'Income Tax Inspection' Louisette believes it was called, where he had to hand in the signed declaration required of all dollar-earning foreigners about to leave the shores of the United States.

The Inspector to whom Francis handed his signed declaration, looked at it for a moment and then turned to the polite but unsmiling colleague sitting at his side.

'This gentleman is a French rose-grower,' he said so significantly that for a moment Francis wondered if even American Income Tax Inspectors preferred tax-payers to have less chancy occupations, ones that made their tax-returns a miracle of simplicity to agree, giving no headaches, no stomach-ulcers to anyone concerned.

But he was mistaken, for the other Inspector looked up and almost smiled.

'Is that so?' he said. 'What's his name?'

'Francis Meilland.'

'Francis Meilland . . .' repeated the second Inspector as if the name rang a bell somewhere in his mind; and he turned to Francis and asked:

'Do you ever come across the man who introduced "Peace" to this country?'

'Sure,' said Francis. 'All the time, in fact. I'm the man.'

It was just as if Francis had uttered some magic 'Open Sesame'. Suddenly away flew all official formality as Francis gathered that both these gentlemen were enthusiastic gardeners and both loved roses above all other flowers. And 'abracadabra!' – no longer were there two polite but highly efficient American Income Tax Inspectors and one French dollar-earner-income-tax-payer; now there were three good gardeners; three ardent rose-lovers chatting most amicably as if over some garden fence, not over an intimidating income-tax desk. And the talk, of course, was all of roses with not one unnecessary word more about taxes.

Louisette says Francis came home full of this chance and friendly encounter. And it wasn't only because one hardly expects the pleasure of talking about roses in an Income Tax Office. No. This meeting meant far more than that to Francis. It happened at the right moment; it was a superb tonic after all the tiring work, the many exhausting journeys he had made to organise 'Universal Rose Selection'. Here they were, two of the unknown millions of rose-lovers he had in mind when he framed that first and all-important aim of 'Universal Rose Selection': 'always to assure greater pleasure, greater satisfaction to anyone who plants a rosebush or buys a rose from a florist'.

But today when Louisette thinks of all that meeting meant to Francis, when she now relives those first years on the Cap d'Antibes, the triumphant birth of Universal Rose Selection, the pace at which they all worked, she is filled with the haunting poignant certainty that Francis felt he must hurry, hurry, that he had not a moment to lose if he was to achieve all he had set his heart on, transmute his plans for the future, his dreams, into reality.

How else explain all they managed to achieve in so few years? It was as if Francis fired them all with his eager, white-hot enthusiasm, his quick vivid imagination, his burning energy. And in record time they had everything so well-organised, so well-equipped that visitors from all over the world began to arrive to see for themselves their new greenhouses in which they now planted many thousands of delicate new rose-seedlings in long concrete bunks, each about ten inches deep, and all of a convenient height so as to cut out unnecessary, back-breaking stooping. These bunks were filled with coarse, clean sand through which circulated precisely the right amount of feeding solution; in short it was rather like bringing up delicate babies on the bottle, but highly scientific bottles filled with the exact amount of carefully balanced food.

Nothing whatever was left to chance in those greenhouses: air, temperature, humidity, everything was automatically controlled and constantly checked. And Papa Meilland strolling around those sand-filled bunks, and looking at the thousands of new rose-seedlings blissfully growing away in them, would often think of the old days up there at Tassin near Lyons, when they had to dig over and prepare some spare patch of ground to plant a 'trial bed' of fifty or so seedlings. And know all the while they would be fortunate indeed if a handful survived.

He would remember again that memorable day . . . how long ago it seemed now! . . . when Monsieur Mallerin had written to say he was bringing the famous American rose-grower, Mr. Robert Pyle, to Tassin later in the week so that he might take a look at the work the promising young French hybridist, Francis Meilland, was now doing. The weather just then, if you remember, had been atrocious, and Papa Meilland and Francis had rushed out into the garden and hastily rigged up a little canopy to protect a small 'trial bed' of fifty new rose-seedlings from the driving wind and rain. And very woebegone they had looked, too, those fifty frail rose-seedlings, but they were all Francis had to show for many months of hard, patient work, and as they rigged up that canopy they prayed they would at least gratefully survive now until Mr. Robert Pyle from America had inspected them.

How everything had changed, thought Papa Meilland. No longer were their seedlings at the ruthless mercy of icy winds, sleet, snow, or sudden night-frosts; or ravenous insects and other devastating pests; or for that matter at the equally devastating mercy of some thrifty dog, like one-eyed Caddy, prowling around looking for a safe handy place to bury a good bone.

No, inside these idyllic greenhouses their delicate rose-seedlings had no rude set-backs whatever; all they had to do was grow, 'en toute béatitude', as Papa Meilland poetically puts it – in most heavenly bliss.

Moreover, it was so very easy and convenient to walk around those sand-filled bunks, decide some baby-rose was ready to be planted outside, give it a gentle tug, and up and out it would come from that coarse, clean sand, all its delicate roots intact, and without disturbing the roots, the beatitude, of its neighbours.

All this scientific simplicity spelt highly organised and inspired planning, of course, and long hours of hard work. Yet Francis still found the energy, the time, to go on with the fight for justice to hybridists. They were legally protected now in America and France, but nowhere else in the world. So Francis studied international law; he digested heavy volumes of the intricate laws governing the granting of patents in other lands. And found they were all different, infuriatingly different; no two countries seemed to have the same ideas, much less the same regulations.

In fact, as Papa Meilland sums it up, one needed the courage of Saint George even to consider tilting against such a battalion

of tricky legal dragons. Not to mention the way one's hair
stood on end to consider what it would cost, for they would
have to engage foreign lawyers, of course, ones who specialised
in everything to do with the granting of patents in their native
lands.

But now Francis had excellent allies – all the members of
Universal Rose Selection were solidly behind him; and with
their help and encouragement, he engaged the necessary lawyers
and determinedly fought many a costly lawsuit in many a
country, repeating over and over again, in one language after
another, the same undeniable facts, setting out the same
conclusive data.

He refused to be discouraged, much less admit he was
beaten even when a lawsuit dragged on and on, and the costs
mounted and mounted, and the law still would obstinately
go on 'supposing' that no hybridist could ever claim to be
a creator.

Many, many a time Francis would remember Mr.
Bumble in Charles Dickens' immortal novel, *Oliver Twist* –
suitable extracts from which Francis had once studied at
those English Language and Literature Evening Classes at
Lyons.

'If the law supposes that,' said Mr. Bumble, . . . ' the law is
a ass – a idiot.'

As the impeccable Professor of the Evening Class had conscientiously pointed out, Mr. Bumble did not precisely speak
'the Queen's English', but he nevertheless most tersely ad-
vanced a considered opinion; an opinion Francis often secretly
yearned to express himself. But he gamely fought on, and by
1954 he had been victorious in Belgium, Germany, Spain,
Morocco, Italy and South Africa. All these countries at last
recognised that a hybridist had the right to legal protection,
that he could now be granted a patent for any new plant or

flower he had patiently worked to create. And Francis wrote in his diary:

'If I am very proud to be the spiritual father of the "Peace" rose, I feel in my heart even greater pride to have at last been able to bring the most eminent jurists of these lands to acknowledge a truth which I alone had once recognised and which no one else would admit in spite of all my explanations.'

Much heartened, Francis then turned his attention to British Law, and soon ruefully concluded that when it came to the granting of patents, that splendid crusader, Charles Dickens, had done all hybridists a real service when he put those immortal words in the mouth of his Mr. Bumble.

British Law 'supposed' that hybridists had no need whatever of patents to protect them in Great Britain. They simply had to make a traditional 'gentleman's agreement' with British horticulturists who with traditional love of 'fair play' would then pay them a voluntary percentage on the sales of any new variety of plant or flower. And this, many of the major horticulturists most conscientiously did. But alas for all 'gentlemen's agreements', there were others who declined to 'play cricket' as the British put it, and who by devious means always managed to acquire a small supply of any new variety, and promptly propagate it; and within months they would be selling it by the thousands without offering a gentlemanly penny of the profit they made on it to the man who had slaved for long years, maybe, to breed and perfect it.

But British Law, like Nelson, turned a blind eye on what it did not wish to behold, and it went on blandly 'supposing' that a 'gentleman's agreement' was perfectly adequate for any hybridist. It also turned a deaf ear to the gentlemen among British horticulturists who had long been demanding new legislation to put an end to this bare-faced and un-British profiteering by pirates on the patient work of others. Now much encouraged by the successful battles fought and won by Francis in Europe, they had legal precedents – even if they were foreign – to flourish in the face of Authority, and quite rightly demanded to know if Great Britain was to lag behind these other civilised countries in the granting of cast-iron patents to protect the work of hybridists.

But the mills of British Law, like the 'mills of God', grind slowly; nevertheless, one respected them, so one hoped, and fought determinedly on.

You must not imagine that new roses, protected by profitable patents in many lands, now began to roll out from the greenhouses and 'trial beds' on the Cap d'Antibes as reguarly and automatically as if from some highly efficient production belt.

Nothing could be further from the truth. As Papa Meilland will tell you, one may have idyllic conditions, employ all the latest techniques, but it still takes time and infinite patience, and the eyes the good God has given a man, to breed any worth-while new rose. Moreover, no scientific methods can predict yet the results of any cross-pollination, no matter how carefully and expertly one selects a pair of parent-roses.

Indeed, to Papa Meilland's mind, this is why the most moving, the most exciting moment is always the one when they see the 'first-born', the first flowers of a new family of tiny rose-plants. In the old days, when they lost so many of their delicate rose-seedlings, they would sometimes dismally wonder if amongst them there had been some miraculously lovely new rose, now lost for ever. But in their idyllic greenhouses all eight hundred or so of a new family would take a firm grip on life, flourish, and burst into bloom.

They would all be different, of course, for now the laws of heredity come into their own – if one can call them 'laws', for as Papa Meilland says every new little rose seems to please itself about which ancestor or ancestors in its long and tangled family-tree it chooses to resemble.

True, this is also the moment when one braces oneself to recognise yet again that most of the eight hundred of every new family will be disappointingly commonplace. But there may be a rare few that take one's breath away. Something in these new roses will have reached far back in time and recaptured some lovely quality of one or the other of their many long-ago, long-forgotten ancestors – an enchanting shape maybe, or some charming colour not seen for many a long year, or best of all to Papa Meilland's mind, so fresh an old-world fragrance that one could easily imagine that not since the days of the rose-loving Empress Josephine had anyone had the delight of holding so fragrant a flower to one's enchanted nose.

Then there may be one or two who inherit more than one wayward trait from some distant ancestors and bloom into downright eccentrics, flaunting gaudy stripes maybe, or bizarre spots. In fact, Papa Meilland says these Bohemians of new roses positively seem to look one straight in the eye and say, 'Well, how's this for heredity?'

On the other hand there may be one new baby rose that will seem to have captured the quintessence of the lovely virtues and qualities of all the most desirable of its ancestors. And up soars one's hopes like milk boiling in a pan.

In short, one never knows what one may see when any new family of baby roses first bursts into bloom. But what one *does* know is that again there can be no short cut. Only time can prove the real value of even the most promising of new roses. Again and again they would 'bud' and plant out some beautiful new rose, optimistically send out supplies of it to all the members of Universal Rose Selection who would equally hopefully plant it out in their 'trial beds' and allow it to grow and prove itself; and this could take anything from five to nine years. And in the end it would fail to come up to its early promise, some disappointing weakness would presently develop, and nothing would come of all the time, care and patience lavished on it.

However, they certainly also had their successes, and these, of course, made them promptly forget all the failures and frustrations. In 1955, for instance, Pepette flung up both arms and at last cried: 'Stupendo! Magnifico!' before one of their new roses. It was a superb geranium red – always a cheerful colour; moreover its stems were long, straight and strong with next to no thorns, and the leaves were a fine glossy green. But what delighted Pepette most of all was the way this new rose burst into blooms that lasted and lasted, not only out there in their gardens under the hot sun of Antibes, but also when cut and arranged in a vase on Memette's table. Furthermore, this obliging rose kept all its freshness and cheerful colour for days on end.

Now Pepette, of course, is always inclined to look at any new rose and consider how it will cut and bunch, how long it will last and give pleasure in a warm room, whereas Papa Meilland always considers how a bush of a new rose will look and give pleasure growing out of doors in someone's garden. And here at last was a new rose that obliged them both; and in a flash someone recalled the French card game: Baccara.

In this game the players, known as the 'pontes', pit their combined luck against one solitary player optimistically styled the 'banquier' – the banker. And on the rare occasion when luck has it that the 'pontes' between them have cards that amount to precisely the same value as those drawn by the 'Banquier', one yells, or politely murmurs – according to one's temperament and environment:

Baccara!

And here was a new rose that seemed to deal Pepette and Papa Meilland cards of equal value. So they promptly called that obliging rose 'Baccara'.

Rose-lovers all over the world were delighted to plant a bush of good-tempered, long-lasting 'Baccara' in their gardens, but it was naturally the florists of the world who received their new rose with open arms; and to-day it is estimated that eighty per cent of the 'cut' roses sold in florists' shops are 'Baccara' – all descended from the one tiny seed, no bigger than a pin's head, that grew into a tiny seedling in those idyllic greenhouses on the Cap d'Antibes, and was then 'budded' and planted out, tested and proved for several years in all the far-flung gardens of Universal Rose Selection.

But between you and him, Papa Meilland says give *him* every time another of that year's successful new roses: a splendid buttercup yellow rose with glossy green leaves and a clean fresh scent with a whiff of lemon-flower about it. At least that's how it smells to Papa Meilland. They called this new rose 'Belle Blonde', and a beautiful and most virtuous blonde it is too, says Papa Meilland, with no connection whatever with the deplorable 'Belle Blonde' gentlemen preferred in that best-seller by an American lady-novelist.

Then there is another of their new roses that is dear to Papa Meilland's heart, maybe because he was born and grew up on a little farm in quiet, unremarkable Chamboeuf, and knows so well what it is to be out and about in the countryside just before daybreak. Suddenly, at the first faint light of dawn, a distant cock will crow, very glad and triumphant, and a moment later from far away in the cool misty dawn, he will be answered by another, and then another. And all the sleeping birds will stir and awake and at once burst into song; and only those who have known that lovely moment of daybreak can know the strange moving wonder of that first distant cock crow and that rapturous dawn-chorus as the fresh new day breaks over the world.

And this new little rose seemed to Papa Meilland to have something of the fresh innocent gaiety of dawn about it; and the name for it, too, came in a flash:

Cocorico!

And why 'Cocorico'? Well, Papa Meilland admits that English-crowing cocks are reputed to call 'Cock-a-doodle-oo!' but he wouldn't know, he's never yet had the pleasure of hearing them; but as every child in France will tell you, all French cocks greet the dawn with a joyous Gallic:

'Co-co-ri-co! Co-co-ri-co!'

If ever you yourself are up and about in the French countryside just before daybreak, then you, too, will most surely hear it, says Papa Meilland, from far, far away at first, then closer and closer as if every cock on all the farms around were greeting one another and the shining new day with that triumphant 'Cocorico!' – the very name for that merry fresh little rose.

Ah yes, they certainly had their triumphs; in fact, it may be said that year after year they saw the success and the launching on the world market of a small but excellent selection of new roses, all tested and approved by the members of Universal Rose Selection.

As you may imagine with every day of the week always packed to overflowing, the hours would fly by so fast that it would seem no time at all before the month of May came round again; and their greenhouses and gardens and house on the Cap d'Antibes would once more echo to the sound of voices speaking many languages. And again Louisette, now with Memette's expert help and advice, would plan and serve excellent and festive meals for the members of 'Universal

Rose Selection', who had come from far and wide for their annual conference. But now there were twenty-five of them, a veritable 'United Nations of Rose-growers' as Francis happily said, and now literally 'universal', for between them they had rose-gardens all over the world.

As the years sped by, the two children began to share that red-letter day in May every year. Michèle would help to serve the coffee and Alain would be at his father's side and all their visitors would exclaim how they had grown, and pay charming little compliments in many languages to Michèle, and agree that Alain absolutely staggered them; he was the very image of his father and so knowledgeable, so excellently informed about their new roses. And so clearly head over heels in love with roses as well – the up and coming fifth generation of a whole family tree of rose-growers and rose-lovers.

It was cruel, tragic; but it was now when both children were growing into all a father could wish, when 'Universal Rose Selection' had become a world-famous reality after so many years of dedicated hard work, when the future shone so full of promise, that suddenly the blackest, the most menacing of clouds threatened all their happiness.

Francis had never been physically strong: if you remember he had been turned down by the French Army when the Second World War broke out. But he himself never permitted anyone to remember this; indeed, it was hard to imagine it, he was always so full of nervous energy, so quick and active, so gay, always bubbling over with eager enthusiasm. 'He lives on the mountain tops,' the well-known and discerning English rose-grower, Harry Wheatcroft, once said of him. But now Francis began to show alarming signs of strain and fatigue. They tried to re-assure themselves, and one another, by saying this was not surprising. Indeed, what else could one expect?

'Whenever One Thinks of Roses'

He had worked so long, so hard, and far too fast for far too many years. And they begged him to rest.

But soon their hearts grew heavy indeed. Fatigue, strain, were not the reason. Francis was ill, gravely ill. A good rest was essential but this alone could never cure him.

Their own family doctor was kindness itself, but he did the only sensible merciful thing – he made an urgent appointment for Francis to go straight to Paris and see a famous specialist. A cancer specialist.

Louisette, of course, went with him, and when they were shown into the specialist's waiting-room, she could hardly believe her eyes. There, on a desk in the corner facing them, was a magnificent vase of roses – 'Peace' roses.

For the first time in weeks, Louisette felt her heart lift. It was so unexpected, as if those well-loved roses were meant for them alone, as if they were there to comfort, reassure them.

She turned to Francis, but the eager words died in her throat as she saw his face and all she could stammer was:

'Mais . . . mais . . . qu'as-tu?'

He did not seem to hear her. He did not even seem to see the roses. Still and silent he stood there, his thin tired face transformed, suddenly radiant with a strange, a heart-breaking emotion.

Then the door opened; the silence was shattered, and a polite voice was asking them please to come this way, the specialist was now ready to receive them.

It was days later before Francis at last replied to that anxious 'Mais . . . qu'as-tu?'

'Louisette,' he said, 'that day we went to see the specialist, I heard you ask me what was the matter. So I knew you only saw the roses in the waiting-room.

'Louisette, it wasn't only the roses waiting for us there. My mother was there. She was standing there, by the side of her roses, smiling at me. I saw her, Louisette. I saw her clearly, so very clearly.'

Louisette has never before told this to anyone. But as the years go by, she still cannot persuade herself that this was the poignant illusion of a man who knew he was most desperately ill.

Not when she remembers the emotion on Francis's face; his quiet, controlled voice repeating:

'I saw her clearly, so very clearly.'

She is convinced that on that day Francis did, indeed, see the mother he loved so dearly standing there by the roses he had dedicated to her memory. And in this he most surely found help, courage and faith to face the desolate days to come.

Everything humanly possible, all their love could do, was done for Francis, but he was never to recover. He died in June, 1958, when the roses were at their loveliest. And all their friends and neighbours, as if sensing what was in Louisette's heart, stripped their gardens of 'Peace' roses, and it was with 'Peace' roses all about him, nothing but 'Peace' roses, that Francis was laid to rest on June 15th in the peaceful cemetery of Antibes. He was only forty-six.

As always in France, there were many moving farewell speeches, many a tribute paid, as the mourners stood about his open grave. Harry Wheatcroft, the English rose-grower, was there with the other members of Universal Rose Selection, and he suddenly realised that he had promised to speak for them all. But he had not realised it would be *there* he must speak – not before that rose-filled grave. However, emotion and grief made him sum up in one brief sentence all that was in their hearts:

'To-day we mourn the passing of a dear friend, one whose

labours have added beauty and fragrance to the gardens of the world, and whose name will forever rank among the greatest of our time whenever one thinks of roses.'

Harry Wheatcroft was right. The name of Francis Meilland will indeed be remembered whenever one thinks of roses. The little boy who had once helped his courageous mother to push a heavy hand-cart laden with vegetables along the country road, who had picked and made neat little bunches of chickweed to sell at the market, had given the world the well-loved 'Peace' rose and many other lovely and dependable new roses.

But surely, also, it will be the hybridists of the future who will remember his name with gratitude.

In 1961, three years after his death, an international convention was signed in Paris, and to-day, thanks to that international agreement, almost all over the civilised world any new variety of plant or flower can be patented, protected legally; and so bring in a just share of all the profits made on it to the man who had the imagination, the skill, the long devoted patience to create it. Three years later Great Britain, too, acknowledged the justice of this, and a new Plant Varieties and Seeds Act came into force, and so at last outlawed all ungentlemanly but profitable piracy.

Francis was not there to see the triumphant realisation of the ideal that had burned so long in his heart and mind, but make no mistake about it, it was he who did all the first heavy spade-work to bring about this triumph. It was his vision, his blazing belief in justice, his incessant hard work that won those first decisive battles, and made possible that final triumph over all mountainous legal obstacles to justice for hybridists.

And as Papa Meilland says, if faith and work were able to move that man-made mountain, why not all other man-made mountains that still bar the way to understanding and justice between nation and nation.

No need, indeed there *are* no words that can tell how Francis was missed by them all at every turn, every hour of the day. But how could they sit back, lost in selfish grief, and see all his plans, his hopes, all he had achieved grow cold, grey, and fruitless?

Alain was only eighteen and his heart was set on roses, on going on with all his father had so brilliantly organised and achieved. So for his sake, and their own, they gathered up the threads and set to work.

Presently Louisette began to sleep a little better at night, and not because she had made herself tackle so long a day's work in the home, office and greenhouses – work in itself is no soporific; but because her desolate heart cried out that she must find the courage to live with sorrow, to turn and not see him there.

Francis had only to come into a room and it would seem to light up. They had understood each other so well. 'Louisette,' he would say, 'it's all hard work now, but you'll see, it will all be so worth-while. Once we have everything organised and the children are older, we'll go everywhere together. Everywhere. You, too, must go round the world – and with me.'

But now . . .

But now she must stifle her anguish, avoid self-pity at all costs. And Louisette would pray for help. She knew what she must do, what Francis would wish, expect her to do. She must keep a kind and welcoming home around her, not only for their children but also for Papa Meilland, now stunned, shattered with grief for the second time in his life.

And in the days, the years, that followed, Louisette summoned up all her courage, and did just that.

'Whenever One Thinks of Roses'

This, however, will hardly surprise you for you will have noticed by now what a golden part women play in all this family story: good Madame Mivière, Grand'mère Jenny and Claudia up there near Lyons; and down there on the Cap d'Antibes Mamma Paolino, little Memette, and Louisette – to this very day, most certainly, Louisette.

CHAPTER FOURTEEN

Cap d'Antibes To-day

To-day Universal Rose Selection is recognised as unique in the long and fascinating history of the rose. This 'United Nations of Rose-growers', as Francis once so proudly and happily called it, now has 'trial beds' in almost every land where roses grow; and the centre of research into the creation and perfecting of new and lovelier roses is still down there, where it began, on the sunny Cap d'Antibes.

In short, everything is going just as Francis planned and toiled so hard to organise and establish.

As for the family, well, let us courteously begin with the oldest-established rose-grower on the Cap d'Antibes – Monsier Francesco Paolino to strangers, but Pepette, of course, to everyone else. At crack of dawn every day of the week you will still find him working in his impeccable greenhouses among his long-stemmed, long-lasting roses. Mamma Paolino's 'tròppo piccolo, tròppo gracile' son is now the youngest eighty-two-year-old you ever set eyes on, fit as a fiddle, and brown as a nut – still conscientiously protected no doubt by Mamma Paolino's favourite saints from the dangers of all that fresh air and sunshine down there on the Cap.

He is also full of plans for his youthful future. For instance, Alain recently spent a holiday in Calabria and came home positively lyrical about the magnificent scenery there and the friendliness of the people he met. Whereupon, Pepette demanded to know what else had his grandson expected – brigands 'infesting' every mountainside? And added that he himself has never had the time yet to make a sentimental journey back to Calabria but that he most certainly will do – one of these days. But not this year, as he has to superintend the installation of a new vat for next year's wine, one of his own design and precise specifications. One has to keep an eye on all this, oneself.

All of which makes Memette throw up both arms and demand to know just what age Pepette imagines himself to be.

But Memette herself is as lively, as warmly hospitable as ever, still forever rolling up her sleeves to prepare yet another of her famous 'pasta asciuttas', and naturally expecting everyone to sit down when it's done to a turn and enjoy it, pronto!

Memette rarely stirs these days, however, from their own home and garden. As she says, why should she? Louisette and the family only live a stone's throw away, and one or the other, or all of them, not to mention many an old friend, are always dropping in to see her. So you see she *has* to be home or she'd miss them.

The truth is, of course, that it is wonderful to sit on the shady terrace outside their comfortable home, looking down over the rose-gardens to the warm blue sea and drink a cup of coffee and talk to little Memette.

Above all, about the old days. Back then roll the years and clearer than yesterday Memette will again make you see them: the scented mountains of flowers in the Perfumery of Grasse; the young ladies of Madame Rondel's impeccable Ironing Establishment, all bursting into shrill sentimental song as the clock struck the last note of eight of an evening, never a second before, and even then keeping one awed, respectful eye on stately Madame Rondel, who had once had the honour of ironing the linen of Her impeccable Majesty, sad, dignified, little Queen Victoria.

Sooner or later, of course, Memette will always come to Mamma Paolino, who had toiled and saved, and seen to it that all the other Paolinos by birth or marriage also toiled and saved to buy some of the wild rough land, the dirt-cheap land, on which their greenhouses and gardens now stand. But that land is no longer dirt-cheap. Ah no, far, far from it.

And thinking of Mamma Paolino, Memette will wipe her eyes and declare that every Paolino by birth or marriage now thanks God for Mamma, a real financial genius if ever there was one, and a great-hearted, loving saint of a mamma – even if the memory of those mass-produced Paolino dresses still lingers on.

Then Memette and Pepette are naturally very proud of their grandchildren: Alain and Michèle. Just to look at Alain, says Memette, just to listen to him, and one sees and hears Francis, his gifted Papa. And Pepette will tersely add that Alain has not disappointed them.

Alain most certainly has not. It is not astonishing, of course, that he has inherited so real a love for roses from both sides of the family, but it is amazing, and indeed poignant, to see how he has also inherited all Francis's vision and drive, his joyous zest for the work he is doing, so that the name of Alain Meilland is rapidly becoming as well known as that of his father, Francis.

As for Michèle, she did precisely what Memette has always prophesied. She shot up at the gallop just as Louisette, her Maman, had done, and Memette could hardly believe her eyes and ears when there was Michèle, grown-up, falling in love, and firmly deciding it was time she married. Or as Pepette chooses to put it, down from Tassin near Lyons again came yet another young brigand of a rose-grower, and carried off his one and only grand-daughter.

But this time, that young brigand of a rose-grower was none other than the very likeable son of their friend and partner, Monsieur Francisque Richardier, who, if you remember, had staggered Papa Meilland and Francis by soberly suggesting they ought to retain a half interest when they offered to sell him their business and gardens at Tassin near Lyons. They had gladly agreed and up had gone that new sign: Meilland-Richardier Establishment – much to the secret comfort of Papa Meilland.

So family history certainly repeated itself; for just like Louisette, her mother, before her had done, Michèle went off with her rose-grower to live among roses near Lyons, or as that poetical guest at Louisette's own wedding had declared, the lovely young bride stepped from one world of roses to another. Which, as Michèle herself dryly observes, was just as well for how on earth else could either lovely young bride ever have hoped to take part in any family discussion.

Moreover, Michèle and her husband decided to start a family straightaway; and now two lively little grandchildren often come to stay with Louisette and follow her around everywhere as faithfully and lovingly as Alain had once followed Grand'mère Jenny. A real comfort and joy to Louisette, of course. And also to their youthful great-grandparents, Pepette, Memette and Papa Meilland.

So now, with those two lively young Meilland-Richardiers playing around in those rose gardens at Tassin near Lyons, the sign over the gateway is truly a family one. Now it is, indeed, the

Meilland-Richardier Establishment.

Papa Meilland, strolling late in the cool of an evening around the gardens down there on the Cap d'Antibes, will often think of those well-loved gardens up there at Tassin; and then he will look around him at the rose-filled greenhouses, the rose-gardens, now stretching away almost down to the sea; and think of the other rose-gardens all over the world of their friends, the members of 'Universal Rose Selection', and he will be filled with wonder to think how simply, how humbly, it all began.

Seventy or so years ago, there they were, four children all unknown to one another: 'piccolo, gracile' Francesco Paolino, nailed by Mamma Paolino, with the best intentions in the world, to a cobbler's bench, but always dreaming of growing roses, nothing but roses; little Marie-Elisabeth Greco carrying round baskets of jasmine in the Perfumery of Grasse and wrinkling her dainty little nose and deciding roses were far more romantic than jasmine, indeed, roses were the aristocrats of all scented flowers; Claudia Dubreuil stealing down the stairs and out into the dawn and her father's gardens on the outskirts of Lyons to cut and bunch roses with the dew still on them to sell at the market on the Quai Saint Antoine, and he himself, Antoine Meilland of the quiet, unremarkable village of Chamboeuf, a noisy young scamp, only silent and still when lost in wonder and love before the beautiful old roses that grew in good Madame Mivière's garden.

How strange to stand back now, as it were, and consider how those four children had been brought together, and linked for ever in one family – all by love of the rose.

And they say there is no romance in life! What nonsense, what dreary nonsense!

Then Papa Meilland will look down on his blue drill jacket and trousers and admit to himself that he may now be taking a few sizes ampler than he did sixty or so years ago, but there he is, thank God, still wearing his gardener's outfit and putting in a full day's work in the gardens or greenhouses. And coming from Chamboeuf, he is not given to easy exaggeration – he may be over eighty now, but in all modesty the eyes the good God has given him are still in excellent shape. And when the time comes round to select the most promising among the many thousands of new roses they now grow every year, well, Papa Meilland has, of course, had a life-time of experience, but it still is very pleasant, if not one hundred per cent accurate, to hear his grandson, Alain, now declare that he, Papa Meilland, never makes a mistake, never!

As for 'retiring, taking a well-earned rest', no thank you, not for Papa Meilland. He still remembers his courageous old mother, Grand'mère Jenny – the very first time she took a rest, she died of it.

Then Papa Meilland will look up at the stars beginning to dance in the deep velvet sky; and stoop to smell a rose. And again the old delight and wonder will fill his heart; and the years will roll back and he will see himself again on that long-ago day of his First Holy Communion in his first brand-new suit, clutching a tall candle, and all unknown to Grand'mère Jenny, that shining new budding-knife carefully stowed away in his trouser pocket.

And he hears again the voice of Monsieur their good Curé, preaching away most beautifully, making all the mothers wipe their eyes. But he himself had not listened, he had not heard one single word – not after the first sentence or so. He had been far, far away, busily planting the shining spaces of heaven with beautiful roses, regardless of cost, all chosen from the sober little rose-catalogues so kindly lent to him by good Madame Mivière.

Ah well, Papa Meilland is not the man to delude himself – he *is* well over eighty now, even if some kind people ask to be permitted to inspect his birth-certificate before they believe this. So it is only salutary at quiet moments like this to think of the hereafter.

Cap d' Antibes To-day

But God is good, and if Papa Meilland merits one day to enter heaven then it will be just as he saw it on that solemn long-ago day.

Heaven without roses? Unthinkable! Of course there will be roses, all the most beautiful of roses blooming celestially to the glory of God. And so Heaven in Excelsis to Papa Meilland.

And Heaven in Excelsis too, please God, to the rest of us, the millions of us the world over who also dearly love a rose.

It is inevitable that the story of any family becomes more and more of a tangle as one generation follows another. So to avoid any undue confusion in this true story of four generations of rose-lovers and rose-growers, here is their

WHO'S WHO

NEAR LYONS

Joseph Rambaux: a gardener by day in the Tête d'Or Park but a dedicated rose-grower in all his free time.

Francis Dubreuil: Joseph's son-in-law. A tailor who, thanks to Joseph, became a first-class professional rose-grower.

Claudia Dubreuil: Francis Dubreuil's daughter.

Antoine Meilland: now known as Papa Meilland, a rose-grower by vocation from the age of eleven. Married Claudia Dubreuil.

Grand'mère Jenny: Antoine Meilland's mother.

Francis Meilland: Antoine and Claudia's son, a brilliant hybridist who gave the world 'Peace' and many other well-loved roses. Founder of UNIVERSAL ROSE SELECTION.

IN ANTIBES ON THE COTE D'AZUR

Papa the Corporal: the head of a large family of Paolinos.

Mamma Paolino: his wife and the financial genius of the family.

Who's Who

Francesco Paolino: their son, a reluctant cobbler who became a most joyous professional rose-grower. Now known to everyone as Pepette.

Marie-Elisabeth Paolino: (née Greco)   Francesco's wife. Now known to everyone as Memette.

Louisette Meilland: (née Paolino)   Pepette and Memette's daughter, their only child, and the wife, now the widow of Francis Meilland.

Louisette's marriage to Francis Meilland linked the two families. The two children of this marriage are:

Alain Meilland: an outstanding young hybridist and dedicated rose-lover. Now ably takes his father's place in UNIVERSAL ROSE SELECTION.

Michèle Richardier: (née Meilland)   Michèle's young husband is a first-class professional rose-grower at Tassin, near Lyons – where this story began!